Derby Days: Fierce Rivalries That Shaped Football

Gigi Romano

Derby Days: Fierce Rivalries That Shaped Football

First Edition: **April 2025**

Table of Contents

Chapter 1: Introduction – The Passion of Derby Days

From the roar of the crowd to the palpable tension that hangs in the air moments before kickoff, few spectacles in sport evoke as much raw emotion and unbridled passion as a football derby. In cities where football is woven into the very fabric of daily life, these clashes become more than just matches—they evolve into epic narratives that define local identity, spark fierce rivalries, and leave an indelible mark on history.

Derby days are unique. They bring together communities bound by a shared heritage and an unwavering devotion to their club. Whether it is the pride of a neighborhood or the deep-rooted traditions passed down through generations, each derby carries with it a legacy that is as much about the people as it is about the sport. On these days, the stadium becomes a stage where the drama of life unfolds: hope, despair, triumph, and heartbreak are all on display, united by a singular focus on victory.

What sets derbies apart is not just the intensity of the game but the stories that have been built around them. Rivalries that have simmered for decades are reignited with every encounter, each contest steeped in history, mythology, and personal memory. The tales of legendary matches, the unforgettable performances of iconic players, and the moments of controversy that have shaped the narrative are passed from one generation to the next, fueling an ever-burning passion for the game.

In these pages, we embark on a journey through the electrifying world of football rivalries. We will delve into the origins and evolution of these intense matchups, explore the cultural and social forces that drive them, and shine a light on the personalities—both on and off the pitch—that have defined these clashes. This book is an ode to the spirit of the derby: a celebration of the raw, untamed energy that fuels a sport beloved around the globe.

As we begin our exploration, it becomes clear that a derby is not simply a game; it is an experience—a tapestry of emotion, pride, and identity. It is a day when allegiances are declared with unwavering certainty and where every pass, tackle, and goal is imbued with meaning. Here, amidst the chants and cheers, lies the heartbeat of football itself—a pulse that has resonated through the ages, uniting fans and communities in a shared celebration of life's most exhilarating moments.

Welcome to *Derby Days: Fierce Rivalries That Shaped*

Football. In the chapters that follow, we will uncover the stories behind some of the most iconic derbies in the UK and Europe, and in doing so, reveal how these monumental clashes have not only shaped the destiny of clubs but also carved out a unique space in the cultural landscape of the modern world.

Chapter 2: The Historical Roots of Rivalry

In the earliest days of organized football, when the sport was still finding its identity, rivalries began to form out of necessity, geography, and a burgeoning sense of community pride. The seeds of these fierce confrontations were sown in small towns and burgeoning industrial centers, where the local club often represented more than just a team—it embodied the hopes, dreams, and even the struggles of its people.

During the late 19th and early 20th centuries, as industrialization transformed cities across the United Kingdom and Europe, football emerged as a powerful social force. Communities that once relied on local trades and familial networks found a common identity in their football clubs. Matches were more than sporting events; they were social gatherings that provided an outlet for local pride and competition. In these crowded urban landscapes, the clubs became a symbol of community spirit, and any contest against a neighboring town or rival district was an opportunity to assert one's identity and independence.

The roots of rivalry were deeply intertwined with the economic and social realities of the time. As industrial fortunes fluctuated, football clubs became beacons of hope amid uncertainty. In cities divided by class, religion, or even linguistic differences, matches often mirrored broader societal divides. The passion on the pitch was fueled by the frustrations and aspirations of the working class, with each derby offering a chance for a moment of triumph in an otherwise challenging daily life. These early rivalries were not merely about scoring goals—they were about proving worth, reclaiming dignity, and challenging the established order.

Historical events, too, played a pivotal role in intensifying these rivalries. The scars of industrial decline, political upheavals, and regional disputes found their way into the narrative of local football. A match could serve as a proxy battle, a safe arena in which rival communities could confront long-standing grievances and assert their unique identity. The intense atmosphere that pervaded these games was a direct reflection of the turbulent times in which they were played—a mirror to the social, economic, and political challenges that defined entire generations.

As football evolved into the modern era, these historical rivalries took on a mythic quality. Stories of past glories and bitter defeats were passed down from one generation to the next, each retelling adding layers of complexity and emotion. These narratives not only honored the achievements of bygone eras but also solidified the identity of the clubs and their supporters. The legends and lore that emerged from these formative years continue to influence the spirit of rivalry, ensuring that every match is steeped in a deep and enduring history.

In tracing the historical roots of rivalry, we uncover not just the evolution of a sport, but the transformation of a community. The intense passions that define derby days are a legacy of times when football was more than a game—it was a battleground for identity, honor, and pride. This chapter sets the stage for our exploration of how these early sparks ignited the flame of rivalry, illuminating the path from modest beginnings to the grand spectacles that now capture the hearts of millions.

Through the lens of history, we see that the origins of football rivalries are not confined to the modern age. They are woven into the very fabric of our cultural and social evolution—a testament to the power of sport to unite, divide, and ultimately define the human experience.

Chapter 3: Cultural and Social Dimensions

Football is much more than a game—it is a cultural phenomenon that both reflects and shapes the society in which it is played. In this chapter, we explore the myriad ways in which derby days serve as a mirror to social dynamics, community values, and cultural identity.

The Fabric of Community

At its core, a derby is a manifestation of community pride. Local football clubs often grow out of the neighborhoods that nurture them, and their rivalries are born from the interwoven narratives of their communities. For many supporters, their club is an extension of themselves—a symbol of belonging and a repository for collective memory. On derby day, this connection becomes palpable; families, friends, and entire neighborhoods converge, united by an unspoken bond that transcends mere fandom. The stadium transforms into a communal space where shared history, traditions, and local legends are celebrated and where the everyday challenges of life are momentarily set aside.

Tradition and Ritual

Every derby is steeped in a rich tapestry of traditions and rituals that have been handed down through generations. These customs—be they the singing of historic anthems, the display of cherished banners, or even the unique pre-match routines observed by die-hard fans—serve as a living link to the past. They remind supporters that every match is part of a long, unbroken chain of stories, victories, and defeats. The rituals create a sense of continuity and reinforce the identity of the club and its followers, providing comfort and a shared sense of destiny that unites disparate lives through a common passion.

Social Identity and Rivalry

Derby days are an arena where social identities are both expressed and challenged. The rivalry is rarely confined to the boundaries of the pitch; it spills over into everyday life, influencing local dialects, fashion, and even politics. The pride associated with supporting a club often carries historical connotations—an allegiance that might be linked to class, ethnicity, or regional identity. In this way, a derby is not just a sporting event but also a stage where the cultural and social narratives of a community are contested and reasserted. Each match becomes a symbolic battle where personal and collective identities are on display, and where victory or defeat resonates on a deeply emotional level.

The Role of Local History

Local history plays an integral role in shaping the cultural dimensions of a derby. Many rivalries are rooted in historical events—be they industrial rivalries, political disputes, or longstanding social divides—that have left an indelible mark on the collective memory of a community. These historical undercurrents lend a gravity to every match, transforming each encounter into a reenactment of past glories and conflicts. In cities where historical narratives are cherished, derbies become a forum for the reaffirmation of local heritage and the storytelling of communal identity. This interplay of history and sport enriches the derby experience, imbuing it with layers of meaning that extend far beyond the final whistle.

A Celebration of Diversity

While rivalries might seem to polarize, derby days are also a celebration of diversity. In modern football, clubs are no longer confined to a single geographic or social niche; they represent a mosaic of cultures, backgrounds, and personal stories. Supporters from different walks of life come together under the banner of their club, creating a vibrant tapestry that reflects both the unity and diversity of the community. This diversity enriches the cultural landscape of derbies, as fans bring their unique perspectives, traditions, and experiences to the collective celebration. It is this confluence of differences that often fuels the passion of a derby, making each encounter a dynamic and evolving story of modern identity.

The Broader Social Impact

The cultural and social dimensions of derbies extend well beyond the stadium. These events have the power to galvanize communities, foster social cohesion, and even drive economic development. Local businesses benefit from the influx of fans, while community initiatives and charitable events often find momentum around the excitement of derby days. Moreover, the narratives crafted around these rivalries can have a lasting impact on regional identity, influencing how communities perceive themselves and how they are perceived by outsiders. In many ways, derbies serve as a microcosm of society, encapsulating both the challenges and the triumphs of communal life.

In sum, the cultural and social dimensions of derby days are a testament to the profound impact football has on society. They are not merely contests played on a field, but vibrant, living expressions of community, tradition, and identity. As we continue our exploration of football rivalries, we will see how these elements—rooted in history and enriched by social dynamics—elevate derbies to a form of art that captures the essence of the human spirit.

Chapter 4: The Anatomy of a Derby Day

A derby day is an orchestrated spectacle—a day when every element, from the early morning anticipation to the final whistle, converges into a powerful narrative of passion and rivalry. In this chapter, we dissect the anatomy of a derby day, exploring each phase as a vital component of an experience that transcends the ordinary and becomes an unforgettable celebration of football.

Dawn of Anticipation

The day begins with an electric undercurrent of excitement that can be felt long before the first fans make their way to the stadium. Local streets come alive with the hum of anticipation as supporters don their team colors, and the air is thick with memories of past glories and heartbreaks. In homes, local pubs, and community centers, discussions of tactics, predictions, and legendary moments create a communal rhythm—a shared heartbeat that pulses with the promise of a historic encounter. This early stage sets the emotional tone for the day, reminding everyone that a derby is not just about sport, but about belonging and identity.

The Journey to the Stadium

The pilgrimage to the stadium is as significant as the

match itself. Whether fans walk, drive, or use public transport, every journey is imbued with ritual and symbolism. Supporters often gather in groups, their collective energy magnifying the significance of the occasion. Along the way, chants, songs, and friendly banter echo through the streets, creating a moving tapestry of sound that underscores the deep-rooted traditions of the rivalry. This procession is more than a commute—it is a mobile celebration of community pride and shared destiny.

The Pre-Match Rituals

Upon arrival at the stadium, the atmosphere shifts into a blend of organized chaos and festive preparation. Fans engage in a series of pre-match rituals that have been honed over decades. Traditional songs and chants are sung with fervor, banners are unfurled, and the air is punctuated by the clamor of horns and drums. Every ritual, from the waving of scarves to the recitation of club anthems, is a deliberate nod to the heritage of the club and the legacy of the rivalry. These customs serve as both a reminder of past glories and a means to unite disparate individuals into a single, impassioned collective.

The Stadium: A Cauldron of Emotion

Stepping into the stadium is like entering a cauldron where raw emotions are concentrated. The design and architecture of these arenas play a pivotal role in amplifying the experience. Close proximity between the stands, the vibrant colors of the fans, and even the acoustics of the stadium all contribute to an immersive environment where every cheer and every groan reverberates with intensity. Here, the stadium transforms into a living, breathing entity—an arena that is as much a character in the story as the teams themselves. It is a space where history is relived in every chant, and where every seat holds the promise of witnessing an extraordinary chapter in the ongoing saga of rivalry.

The Match: A Theatre of Tactics and Emotions

When the match begins, the stadium erupts into a symphony of sound and movement. Every pass, tackle, and goal is not merely a statistic but a narrative moment that encapsulates the spirit of the derby. On the pitch, tactical battles mirror the strategic planning observed by the fans off the field. Managers and players are acutely aware that they are part of a storied legacy, where individual brilliance and collective effort intertwine to create moments of transcendent beauty or crushing despair. The ebb and flow of the game are marked by moments of high drama—nervous pauses before a penalty, the explosive celebration of a goal, and the quiet resignation of a near-miss—all of which contribute to the rich tapestry of the derby narrative.

The Role of the Crowd

No derby day is complete without acknowledging the central role of the crowd. The collective voice of the fans shapes the destiny of the match. Whether it is a raucous cheer that lifts a team to new heights or a tense silence that amplifies the gravity of a critical moment, the supporters are an active, dynamic force. Their energy can sway momentum, inspire extraordinary performances, and sometimes even alter the course of the game. The emotional interplay between the players and the crowd creates a feedback loop that transforms the match into a living dialogue between the field and the stands—a conversation that has been going on for generations.

Post-Match Reflections

When the final whistle blows, the intensity of the derby does not simply dissipate. Instead, the aftermath becomes a period of reflection, celebration, and, at times, commiseration. Fans discuss the highs and lows of the match, dissecting key moments and contemplating what they mean for the future. Whether it is the jubilation of a hard-fought victory or the bitter lessons of a narrow defeat, the post-match period is an essential part of the derby experience. It is a time when emotions are processed and stories are born—stories that will be recounted in pubs, homes, and social media for years to come.

A Living Tradition

Every derby day is a reiteration of a living tradition. The rituals, the journeys, the collective emotions, and the tactical battles are all interwoven into a narrative that is both timeless and continually evolving. Each match writes a new chapter in the long history of the rivalry, ensuring that the legacy of derby days endures, continually renewing the bond between clubs and their supporters.

In essence, the anatomy of a derby day is a celebration of football as a grand theatrical production—a stage where passion, identity, and history are brought together in a display that is as dynamic as it is deeply meaningful. Through every moment of anticipation, every burst of action on the pitch, and every echo of fanfare in the stands, the derby captures the very soul of football, creating memories that resonate long after the day has ended.

Chapter 5: Fan Culture – Voices from the Stands

Football is more than a contest played on the pitch—it is a tapestry woven by the voices, passions, and traditions of its supporters. In this chapter, we delve into the heart of fan culture, exploring the unique rituals, diverse perspectives, and enduring loyalties that animate derby days. This is the realm where personal narratives intertwine with collective memory, and where the power of belonging transforms mere spectators into the lifeblood of football.

The Soundtrack of the Stands

One of the most defining elements of fan culture is the chorus of voices that rises in unison within the stadium. Chants, anthems, and songs are not just background noise; they are an intrinsic part of the derby experience. Each chant is a story—a celebration of past glories, a lament for missed opportunities, or a rallying cry for unity. These vocal expressions serve several purposes: they intimidate rivals, galvanize the team, and create an atmosphere that is both electrifying and intimidating. Whether it is a traditional club anthem passed down through generations or a spontaneous burst of creative expression in response to the ebb and flow of the match, the soundtrack of the stands encapsulates the raw emotion and communal spirit of the fans.

The Art of the Choreography

Beyond vocal expressions, fan culture is distinguished by its elaborate displays and choreographies. From meticulously arranged banners to synchronized movements and light shows, these visual spectacles are designed to transform the stadium into a living canvas of identity and pride. Each display is a carefully crafted message that reflects the club's heritage and the values of its supporters. The artistry involved is not merely decorative—it is a form of storytelling that celebrates the uniqueness of each club and its community. Through these coordinated efforts, fans assert their presence, declare their allegiance, and inscribe their collective memory into the fabric of every derby.

Stories of Loyalty and Identity

At the core of fan culture lies an unwavering loyalty that is often forged in the crucible of personal and communal experience. For many supporters, the connection to their club is a defining aspect of their identity. It is a bond that transcends the boundaries of geography, class, and even time. Stories of lifelong allegiance abound—tales of fathers and sons who have shared countless derby days, of friends who found unity in the shared experience of victory and defeat, and of communities that have rallied together in the face of adversity. These narratives underscore the notion that supporting a club is not a casual pastime but a profound commitment to a way of life. In the stands, every cheer, every tear, and every moment of collective elation speaks to a deep-seated passion that is both personal and universal.

The Social Fabric of the Fan Community

Fan culture is also a microcosm of society—a space where diverse voices come together to form a vibrant, dynamic community. Within the stands, differences in background, opinion, and circumstance converge in a shared celebration of the sport. This diversity is one of the hallmarks of fan culture; it is a melting pot where individuals from all walks of life can find common ground. The sense of belonging that pervades these communities is reinforced by mutual respect and the collective understanding that, despite individual differences, the love for the club unites them all. Social media and digital platforms have further enriched this dynamic, allowing fans to connect beyond the physical confines of the stadium, exchange stories, and preserve the lore of their beloved derbies.

The Passion Beyond the Match

The influence of fan culture extends well beyond the 90 minutes of play. In the aftermath of a derby, the stands become hubs of post-match analysis and reflection. Fans gather in local pubs, community centers, and online forums to dissect every moment of the game—debating tactics, celebrating heroics, and sometimes mourning a narrow defeat. This post-match communion is as integral to the derby experience as the match itself, serving as a space for healing, catharsis, and, ultimately, renewal of the collective spirit. It is in these moments that the true depth of fan culture is revealed—a culture that thrives on discussion, memory, and the eternal hope of future victories.

The Evolution of Fan Expression

While traditional expressions of support remain the backbone of fan culture, modern influences have introduced new forms of expression. Technology has transformed the ways in which fans interact with one another and with the game. Live tweets, real-time match blogs, and digital fan forums have become extensions of the stadium, offering a parallel arena where emotions can be shared instantaneously with a global audience. Yet, despite these technological advances, the core essence of fan culture remains unchanged: a fervent, unyielding passion that finds its roots in community, history, and a deep-seated love for the game.

A Legacy of Voice and Vision

The voices from the stands have always been more than mere spectators—they are the storytellers, the custodians of tradition, and the champions of the club's identity. Their collective roar is a testament to the enduring power of football as a cultural force. In every chant and every display, they remind us that the spirit of the derby is not confined to the pitch but lives on in the hearts of those who believe, year after year, that their club is more than just a team; it is a way of life.

As we turn the page to explore the next chapters of our journey through derby history and culture, let us carry with us the vibrant echoes of fan culture—a reminder that the true soul of football is found in the voices, stories, and shared experiences of its supporters.

Chapter 6: Derby Spotlight – The Merseyside Derby (Liverpool vs. Everton)

Few rivalries in football capture the soul of a city quite like the Merseyside Derby, where the clubs of Liverpool and Everton have clashed for well over a century. This isn't merely a game played on a pitch—it is an enduring saga of passion, pride, and identity that has come to define the very essence of Merseyside.

A Tale Rooted in History

The origins of the Merseyside Derby stretch back to the early days of organized football, when local clubs began to emerge as symbols of community pride. Liverpool FC and Everton FC, both born from working-class neighborhoods, quickly became emblematic of the city's resilience and fierce independence. Over time, this friendly rivalry evolved into one of the most intense and storied derbies in the world, with each match adding new chapters to an already rich historical tapestry. The rivalry is a mirror reflecting the city's own evolution—from a bustling industrial hub to a modern metropolis where tradition and innovation coalesce.

The Spirit of the City

Liverpool is a city where football is interwoven with everyday life. For generations, families have passed down their allegiance from parent to child, and the choice between supporting Liverpool or Everton is often as deeply personal as it is communal. This divide is not born of animosity but of a shared love for the game—a love that is expressed with passion, pride, and a characteristic Merseyside wit. On derby day, the city becomes a vibrant canvas painted in the reds and blues of the two clubs, with every street, pub, and neighborhood buzzing with anticipation.

Iconic Moments and Legendary Encounters

Over the decades, the Merseyside Derby has produced moments that have transcended the boundaries of sport. There have been dramatic comebacks, last-minute winners, and tactical masterclasses that have left an indelible mark on football lore. Whether it's the electric atmosphere at Anfield when the Reds are defending their home turf, or the steadfast resolve of Goodison Park's faithful, every match is a celebration of rivalry and an homage to the spirit of competition. These encounters are often characterized by a blend of high drama and a deep-seated respect—a rivalry where the intensity on the field is matched by a shared understanding of what the derby means to the community.

The Fans: Custodians of Legacy

The true heartbeat of the Merseyside Derby lies with its supporters. The chants, banners, and collective roars of the fans create an atmosphere that is both formidable and deeply moving. Generations of supporters have gathered to witness the unfolding drama, their voices rising in unison to celebrate glory or to console in defeat. In every corner of the stadium, the passion of the fans is palpable—each cheer a reminder of the countless memories forged in the heat of rivalry. For many, the derby is not just a match; it is a ritual, a moment to reconnect with family, history, and the very essence of what it means to belong to Merseyside.

Off the Field: A Cultural Celebration

The impact of the Merseyside Derby extends well beyond the boundaries of the pitch. It has spurred cultural expressions in music, art, and literature, capturing the hearts of those who find in the derby a metaphor for life itself. Local pubs overflow with spirited debates and shared reminiscences, and the city's streets come alive with murals and graffiti that pay tribute to legendary players and unforgettable matches. This cultural celebration reaffirms that the derby is more than a sporting contest—it is a living, breathing narrative that encapsulates the hopes, struggles, and dreams of an entire community.

The Modern Era and the Future

Today, the Merseyside Derby stands as a testament to both tradition and progress. While modern tactics, media, and technology have added new dimensions to the game, the core values that define the rivalry remain unchanged. New generations of fans continue to embrace the legacy of their forebears, ensuring that the spirit of the derby endures. As both clubs evolve, adapting to the fast pace of modern football, the eternal allure of the Merseyside Derby remains a constant—an ever-present reminder of the passion, rivalry, and shared history that continue to shape the landscape of football.

In celebrating the Merseyside Derby, we celebrate more than just two clubs competing on a given day—we honor a legacy of community, pride, and the enduring power of sport to unite and inspire. Each match is a vivid reminder that, in the heart of Merseyside, football is not simply a game; it is a way of life, a story that continues to evolve with every kick, every cheer, and every memory forged on the hallowed grounds of rivalry.

Chapter 7: Derby Spotlight – The Manchester Derby (Manchester United vs. Manchester City)

Few rivalries in modern football encapsulate the dramatic evolution of the sport quite like the Manchester Derby. This fierce contest between Manchester United and Manchester City is not only a battle for local supremacy but also a reflection of the city's transformation—from its industrial roots to its current status as a global hub of business, culture, and innovation.

A Tale of Two Legacies

The story of the Manchester Derby is a tale of two distinct footballing legacies. Manchester United, with its storied history of triumphs on the domestic and European stage, has long been celebrated as a symbol of resilience and global appeal. In contrast, Manchester City's rise from modest beginnings to a powerhouse of modern football speaks to the spirit of reinvention and ambition. Their rivalry, forged on the same soil, embodies contrasting philosophies: the tradition and legacy of United versus the dynamic, forward-thinking approach of City. Over the decades, these differences have fueled an intense rivalry that mirrors the city's own metamorphosis.

Historical Context and Cultural Roots

The rivalry finds its roots in Manchester's rich industrial history. In the early 20th century, both clubs emerged as beacons of local pride, each rallying support from communities that were navigating the challenges of industrial growth and economic uncertainty. As the city evolved, so too did the clubs, with Manchester United growing into a global brand while Manchester City nurtured a passionate local identity. The derby thus became a stage where not only footballing prowess was displayed but also the cultural, social, and economic shifts of Manchester were laid bare.

Iconic Matches and Pivotal Moments

The Manchester Derby has provided football fans with a treasure trove of unforgettable moments. Legendary encounters—marked by last-minute goals, dramatic comebacks, and tactical masterclasses—have etched themselves into the collective memory of the city. Iconic matches such as those featuring brilliant individual performances and strategic brilliance have turned the derby into a recurring epic saga. Each game is not simply a contest for three points; it is a narrative chapter where heroes are made, rivalries deepened, and the destiny of the season is often decided.

The Role of the Fans

At the heart of every Manchester Derby lies the passionate support of its fans. The atmosphere in the stadiums—be it Old Trafford or the Etihad Stadium—is electric, fueled by generations of supporters who live and breathe the rivalry. For the fans, the derby is much more than a game; it is a reaffirmation of identity. The chants, the banners, and the shared emotional highs and lows create a collective experience that binds communities. This passionate support is the lifeblood of the derby, providing both clubs with an indomitable spirit and an enduring sense of purpose.

Off the Field: The Socio-Economic Impact

Beyond the confines of the pitch, the Manchester Derby has a profound impact on the local community and economy. On matchdays, the city transforms as businesses, local media, and even international advertisers converge to celebrate this emblematic event. The derby has spurred cultural expressions through music, art, and literature, capturing the zeitgeist of a city that is both proud of its heritage and eager to embrace the future. This ripple effect of economic and cultural vitality underlines how deeply interwoven football is with the fabric of Manchester.

The Modern Era: Evolution and Rivalry in a New Age

In recent years, the Manchester Derby has taken on new dimensions with the advent of modern football technologies, global broadcasting, and significant financial investments. These factors have intensified the rivalry, as both clubs harness cutting-edge tactics, world-class talent, and innovative strategies to gain an edge on the field. Yet, amid the glitz and glamour of modern football, the derby retains its raw intensity and enduring connection to the city's soul. It is a reminder that beneath the layers of commercial success and technological advancement, the heart of Manchester football still beats to the rhythm of local passion and historical legacy.

Looking to the Future

As the Manchester Derby continues to evolve, its future remains as compelling as its past. The rivalry is poised to grow even more intense as emerging talents, tactical innovations, and shifting global dynamics reshape the landscape of the game. For the supporters, each derby is a reaffirmation of loyalty—a promise that the spirit of the contest will live on, no matter what changes the future may bring. The ongoing saga of the Manchester Derby is not just a chronicle of sporting battles; it is a living narrative of a city that continues to redefine itself, match after match, generation after generation.

In celebrating the Manchester Derby, we witness a microcosm of modern football—a fusion of history, culture, and ambition that captures the imagination of fans around the world. This rivalry, rooted in the past yet ever-adaptive to the present, stands as a testament to the enduring power of sport to inspire, unite, and transform.

Chapter 8: Derby Spotlight – The North London Derby (Arsenal vs. Tottenham Hotspur)

Few rivalries in English football are as charged with emotion and history as the North London Derby between Arsenal and Tottenham Hotspur. This rivalry, which pits two of London's most prominent football clubs against each other, is more than just a game—it is a reflection of the socio-political history of North London, the fiercely competitive spirit of both clubs, and the unique cultural identity that has shaped the supporters of each team.

The Origins of the Rivalry

The origins of the North London Derby are somewhat unconventional, as it wasn't simply a matter of geographical proximity. Arsenal, originally formed as Woolwich Arsenal in 1886, moved to Highbury in North London in 1913, a move that would alter the course of local footballing history. At the time, Tottenham Hotspur was the dominant club in the area, having established itself in the heart of North London for decades. Arsenal's decision to relocate to the area ignited tensions, with some local Tottenham fans perceiving it as an act of encroachment. Over time, what began as a local dispute between clubs morphed into one of the fiercest and most passionately contested rivalries in the world.

As the years passed, both clubs grew in stature, with Arsenal achieving considerable success, particularly in the mid-20th century, and Tottenham also gaining recognition for its attacking style of play and key successes. Yet, the underlying animosity between the two fanbases remained, as the rivalry became about more than just football—it became about pride, status, and identity in North London.

Cultural and Societal Underpinnings

The North London Derby isn't just a rivalry based on footballing achievement; it's deeply intertwined with the social and cultural dynamics of the region. Arsenal, historically associated with the working-class communities in the Highbury area, became a symbol of upward mobility in the face of a rapidly evolving city. The club's success under manager Herbert Chapman in the 1930s set the stage for its rise as one of the dominant clubs in English football.

Tottenham, on the other hand, has long been identified with a more traditional, local identity. The club's origins in the East End of London and later establishment in the area near White Hart Lane imbue it with a sense of pride that is deeply tied to its community roots. Over the decades, Tottenham's working-class support base has remained fiercely loyal, and the club has embodied a spirit of resilience, continuing to fight against the dominance of Arsenal and other top-flight teams.

The rivalry thus became a clash of not just football philosophies but of different social identities. For Arsenal, the move to North London signified a desire to break away from its roots and establish itself as a club with national—and even international—appeal. For Tottenham, it became a struggle to defend its local dominance against a perceived invader. This cultural dynamic added layers of tension to their meetings, as both sets of fans carried with them a deep sense of belonging and pride in their respective clubs.

High-Stakes Encounters: The Games that Defined the Derby

Over the years, the North London Derby has produced some of the most thrilling and dramatic moments in English football. From last-minute goals to thrilling comebacks, the encounters between Arsenal and Tottenham have had a lasting impact on both teams and their supporters.

One of the most iconic moments in the history of the derby occurred in 2004 when Arsenal, led by manager Arsène Wenger, went unbeaten throughout the entire

Premier League season—culminating in a victory against Spurs at White Hart Lane. The match saw the Gunners clinch the title in front of their rivals, adding further fuel to the already fiery rivalry. The symbolism of Arsenal maintaining their undefeated record in such a crucial encounter made the victory all the sweeter for the red half of North London.

For Tottenham, the North London Derby represents their chance to upend their larger rivals. Tottenham's 3-2 victory in 1991, which saw them defeat Arsenal in the FA Cup semi-finals, remains one of the club's most cherished moments in its long history. That victory, coming in a high-stakes knockout competition, cemented Tottenham's resolve as a club capable of taking on its seemingly superior neighbors.

Other matches, such as the infamous 4-4 draw in 2008, have been laced with drama. The game, which saw Arsenal squander a 4-2 lead in the final moments, is often cited as a perfect example of the unpredictable nature of the derby and the emotions that come with it. The atmosphere surrounding these encounters only serves to heighten the stakes, with every goal and every tackle sending ripples of joy or despair throughout the stands.

The Fans: The True Custodians of the Derby

The North London Derby is as much about the fans as it is about the players on the field. In fact, the passion of the supporters often transcends the game itself, as every match provides an opportunity to reaffirm local pride, one's allegiance to the club, and a sense of belonging. The chants, the banners, and the animated debates that follow every encounter are all part of the rich tapestry of fan culture that fuels the rivalry.

For Arsenal supporters, the North London Derby represents not just the chance to beat Tottenham, but also to assert their place at the top of the footballing hierarchy. Arsenal fans take immense pride in the club's history and the successful eras that have defined their identity—especially under Wenger's leadership. The rivalry offers them an occasion to demonstrate their club's superiority over Spurs, not just in footballing terms, but in terms of the broader cultural and social prestige of the club.

For Tottenham fans, the derby provides an annual opportunity to remind the world that they are a force to be reckoned with, despite the overwhelming dominance of Arsenal in the past. For many Spurs supporters, defeating their North London rivals is a form of validation—a chance to prove that they, too, can compete at the highest level. The rivalry allows Tottenham fans to assert their identity, not as mere underdogs but as a club with a rich history, a proud fanbase, and the ambition to stand toe-to-toe with the very best.

The Future of the Rivalry

As football evolves, so too does the North London Derby. Both clubs have experienced periods of transformation, with new ownerships, fresh managerial approaches, and different tactical philosophies coming into play. For Arsenal, the post-Wenger era has presented both challenges and opportunities, while Tottenham, under the leadership of high-profile managers like Mauricio Pochettino and José Mourinho, has developed a more competitive edge, becoming a consistent contender at the top of the league.

The North London Derby's appeal remains as potent as ever, transcending mere football and offering a stage for fans to celebrate their cultural identity, their regional pride, and their club's rich history. As the city of London continues to evolve, the rivalry between Arsenal and Tottenham will remain a central part of its footballing and cultural landscape—a testament to the passion and enduring legacy of one of the fiercest derbies in the world.

In the world of football, rivalries come and go, but the North London Derby stands as a timeless reminder of how a shared history, cultural identity, and passionate support can create a footballing spectacle that continues to captivate and inspire.

Chapter 9: Derby Spotlight – The Old Firm (Celtic vs. Rangers)

Few rivalries evoke as much passion and controversy as the Old Firm derby, where Celtic and Rangers have clashed on the pitch and in the hearts of their supporters for over a century. This rivalry transcends football, weaving together threads of history, religion, and cultural identity into a narrative that is as complex as it is compelling.

Historical Origins and Context

The roots of the Old Firm rivalry can be traced back to the late 19th century, when both Celtic and Rangers were established in Glasgow with very different founding principles. Celtic was founded by Irish immigrants seeking to preserve their heritage and offer support to their community, while Rangers emerged with a distinctly Protestant identity. From these divergent origins, a fierce rivalry was born—one that was as much about cultural and religious identity as it was about sporting excellence. Over the decades, political and social tensions in Scotland only served to deepen this divide, ensuring that every match between the two clubs was laden with historical significance.

As Glasgow evolved into a bustling urban center, the

stakes of the Old Firm rivalry grew ever higher. In an era marked by rapid industrialization and significant social change, the clubs became emblematic of competing visions for Scottish society. Each encounter on the pitch was not merely a contest for supremacy in football but a symbolic battle that reflected the aspirations, prejudices, and hopes of entire communities.

Cultural and Religious Dimensions

At the core of the Old Firm derby lie cultural and religious identities that have defined both clubs for generations. Celtic's association with the Catholic and Irish communities, contrasted with Rangers' Protestant and Unionist roots, has often transformed matches into expressions of deeper, long-standing divisions. This cultural and religious dichotomy has fueled both rivalry and camaraderie, as supporters see in their clubs a representation of their own heritage and values.

The rivalry's cultural impact extends beyond the stadium. In neighborhoods across Glasgow and beyond, the colors of green and white or blue and red evoke not only footballing loyalty but also a sense of belonging to a community with a distinct narrative. Songs, rituals, and even local politics have been influenced by the fervor of the Old Firm, making each derby a poignant reminder of the power of identity in shaping both sport and society.

Iconic Encounters and Rivalry Narratives

Over the years, the Old Firm has produced a wealth of memorable encounters that have entered the annals of football folklore. There have been nights of high drama, where last-minute goals, heated exchanges, and tactical masterstrokes have defined the outcome of a match and, by extension, the mood of an entire season. These iconic fixtures are frequently revisited in both media and memory, with each retelling adding new layers to the narrative.

Stories of legendary performances by Celtic and Rangers players are interwoven with episodes of intense rivalry—matches that were as unpredictable as they were emotionally charged. Whether it's a heroic comeback or a bitter defeat, each game adds to the rich tapestry of the Old Firm, reinforcing the notion that every encounter is a fresh chapter in a long and storied rivalry.

The Fans: A Community Divided and United

The true essence of the Old Firm derby is found in its supporters. The passion of the fans, often expressed in a blend of exuberance and solemnity, gives the rivalry its enduring power. In the stands, chants and songs resonate with the voices of generations who have experienced both triumph and heartbreak. For many, the derby is a pilgrimage—a time when longstanding loyalties are celebrated and, sometimes, tested.

Yet, amid the intensity, there is also a remarkable sense of shared identity. Despite the deep divisions that can surface on derby day, many fans acknowledge the unique role that the Old Firm plays in Scottish culture. The rivalry, with all its complexities, has forged a common narrative that transcends the individual allegiances of its supporters. It is a reminder that football can both divide and unite, capturing the bittersweet essence of community life.

The Modern Era and Contemporary Challenges

In recent years, the Old Firm derby has had to navigate a rapidly changing landscape. Modern football's commercial pressures, increased media scrutiny, and a growing awareness of the social implications of sectarianism have all contributed to a redefinition of the rivalry. Both clubs have invested in modernizing their approaches, striving to balance the rich heritage of the past with the demands of contemporary sport.

This evolution has not been without challenges. Efforts

to curb violence and promote inclusivity have often met resistance from those who view the traditional aspects of the rivalry as inviolable. Nevertheless, there is a growing consensus among many supporters and club officials that the future of the Old Firm lies in embracing change without erasing history. As both Celtic and Rangers look ahead, the hope is that the derby can serve as a model for how sport can reconcile passionate rivalries with the needs of a modern, diverse society.

Legacy and Impact on Scottish Football

The influence of the Old Firm extends far beyond the boundaries of Glasgow. It has shaped the identity of Scottish football, setting standards of excellence, passion, and rivalry that resonate across the nation. The derby has also had a profound cultural impact, inspiring art, literature, and music that capture the essence of Scottish life in its most vibrant and conflicted forms.

In celebrating the Old Firm, we honor not just a football match, but a living tradition that has defined the spirit of an entire people. The legacy of Celtic and Rangers is a testament to the enduring power of sport to encapsulate the joys, sorrows, and complexities of life itself. As the chapters of this rivalry continue to be written, the Old Firm remains a powerful symbol of passion, identity, and the unbreakable bond between a community and its beloved game.

Chapter 10: Derby Spotlight – The Tyne-Wear Derby (Newcastle United vs. Sunderland)

Few fixtures in English football encapsulate raw regional passion and historical intensity like the Tyne-Wear Derby. This storied rivalry between Newcastle United and Sunderland is steeped in local pride, marked by generations of fierce competition and characterized by the deep-seated identity of the North East. More than just a game, the Tyne-Wear Derby is a reflection of the economic, cultural, and social dynamics that have shaped this unique part of England.

A Rivalry Forged in the North East

The origins of the Tyne-Wear Derby lie in the industrial heartlands of North East England. Both Newcastle and Sunderland grew up during the era of coal mining, shipbuilding, and manufacturing, industries that powered the region and instilled a sense of resilience and determination. Football clubs emerged as the beating hearts of their communities, offering a beacon of hope and pride amidst the daily struggles of industrial life. As both cities strove to assert their identity and economic independence, the football pitch became a battleground where local honor was on the line. The rivalry thus evolved into an expression of regional solidarity as much as competitive spirit.

Cultural Identity and Regional Pride

For supporters of Newcastle United and Sunderland, the derby is a celebration of the North East's unique cultural identity. In Newcastle, the Magpies symbolize not only sporting excellence but also the storied history of a city that has long been associated with determination and a fighting spirit. In Sunderland, the Black Cats are equally emblematic—a reminder of the community's enduring commitment to their club against all odds. The clash between these two sides is an annual reaffirmation of regional pride, as each set of fans seeks to prove that their city's legacy and working-class spirit still reign supreme.

The derby transcends the realm of sport; it is a social phenomenon. On matchdays, local pubs, cafes, and streets buzz with anticipatory chatter, as families and friends come together to celebrate a rivalry that has defined local identity for generations. The distinct dialects, traditions, and communal values of the North East find their most passionate expression on derby day, where every cheer and every groan resonates with the echoes of history and local pride.

Iconic Moments on the Pitch

The Tyne-Wear Derby has produced a series of unforgettable moments that have become embedded in the collective memory of both clubs' supporters. Dramatic goals, last-minute heroics, and intense tactical battles have all contributed to a rivalry that is as unpredictable as it is enthralling. Matches have often swung like a pendulum between elation and despair—each game offering a narrative of its own that will be recounted for years to come.

One of the derby's most memorable encounters unfolded in the late 20th century, when a stunning comeback by Sunderland against a dominant Newcastle side became the talk of the region. Such moments have not only defined individual matches but have also elevated the derby into a near-mythical status—a testament to the enduring spirit of competition and the ever-present possibility of glory. Each game serves as a reminder that in the Tyne-Wear Derby, anything can happen, and every minute on the pitch is imbued with historical weight.

The Passionate Supporters

At the heart of the Tyne-Wear Derby lies its fans—the lifeblood of the rivalry. Newcastle supporters, known for their fervent loyalty and raucous displays at St. James' Park, contrast vividly with the impassioned followers of Sunderland, who fill the Stadium of Light with chants, banners, and a palpable sense of determination. For these fans, the derby is a ritual that transcends the boundaries of time and space—a yearly celebration of their city's heritage and an affirmation of their unwavering commitment to their club.

The intensity of the fans' emotions can be felt long before kickoff and lingers long after the final whistle. In homes and local gathering spots, the derby becomes a shared experience—an opportunity for old rivalries to be both reignited and reconciled through the communal act of supporting their team. The stories passed down through generations, of miraculous victories and heart-wrenching defeats, add layers of meaning to the derby, ensuring that every match is as much about history and identity as it is about the present contest.

Beyond the Field: Social and Economic Impact

The influence of the Tyne-Wear Derby extends well beyond the confines of the football stadium. On matchdays, the entire region feels the economic and social ripple effects of this storied rivalry. Local businesses see a surge in activity as fans flock to pubs, restaurants, and retail outlets, all eager to share in the collective celebration and commiseration that the derby brings. Moreover, the derby acts as a catalyst for community bonding, sparking conversations, debates, and, at times, even charitable initiatives that strengthen the social fabric of the North East.

The derby has also inspired a rich tradition of local art, literature, and music—creative expressions that capture the unique flavor of the rivalry. From graffiti murals celebrating past heroes to folk songs that echo through the narrow streets of Sunderland and Newcastle, the cultural imprint of the Tyne-Wear Derby is indelible. It is a reminder that, for many in the North East, football is not simply a pastime but a vital part of their collective identity.

Looking Ahead

As both Newcastle United and Sunderland navigate the challenges of modern football—balancing tradition with the demands of commercialization—the Tyne-Wear Derby remains a timeless symbol of regional pride and fierce competition. While tactics and technologies may evolve, the core spirit of the derby endures: a burning desire to honor the legacy of the past while forging a path toward future glory.

In celebrating the Tyne-Wear Derby, we recognize not just a football match but a cultural phenomenon that has shaped, and continues to shape, the identity of an entire region. The passion, history, and unyielding loyalty of its supporters ensure that every derby is more than a game—it is an enduring saga of community, resilience, and the relentless pursuit of pride.

Chapter 11: Derby Spotlight – The Milan Derby (Inter Milan vs. AC Milan)

Few football rivalries embody both the glamour and intensity of Italian football as powerfully as the Milan Derby. The clash between Inter Milan and AC Milan—often referred to as the "Derby della Madonnina"—transcends sporting competition to become a cultural spectacle, steeped in history, local pride, and a dazzling display of footballing artistry.

A Tale of Two Legacies

The Milan Derby is a unique contest between two clubs that share not only the same city but also the iconic San Siro stadium, where each match is a battle for supremacy on home turf. AC Milan, known for its elegant style and storied European successes, has long been a symbol of Italian flair and global ambition. In contrast, Inter Milan, with its fierce competitiveness and a rich history of domestic triumphs, embodies a more pragmatic, hard-fought approach to the game. This duality—grace versus grit—creates a compelling narrative, one where each encounter is a stage for contrasting footballing philosophies that have evolved over decades.

Historical Context and Cultural Significance

The rivalry between Inter and AC Milan dates back to the early 20th century, when both clubs were established as pillars of the Milanese community. Their shared history is interwoven with the city's evolution into a modern metropolis, reflecting Milan's transformation from an industrial hub to a global center of fashion, design, and business. The derby is not merely a contest for points; it is a celebration of Milan's cultural identity, a moment when the city's heritage is put on full display through the passion and pride of its supporters.

The "Derby della Madonnina" derives its name from the statue of the Virgin Mary that crowns the Milan Cathedral, a symbol that resonates deeply with the people of Milan. This religious and cultural icon underscores the derby's significance beyond football—a reminder that the rivalry is as much about community identity and tradition as it is about the sport itself.

The Theatre of San Siro

San Siro is more than just a stadium—it is a cauldron of emotion, history, and anticipation. Sharing this iconic ground, both Inter and AC Milan have created a formidable atmosphere that amplifies the drama of the derby. On matchday, the stadium transforms into a vibrant arena where the thunderous applause, rhythmic chants, and synchronized displays of support merge into a singular expression of Milanese passion.

Every corner of San Siro is steeped in memories of past glories and heartbreaks. The stadium's architecture, with its imposing stands and sweeping curves, serves as a fitting backdrop for a rivalry that is as visually and emotionally captivating as the game itself. Whether it's the blinding flashes of cameras capturing a moment of individual brilliance or the collective roar of the crowd following a decisive goal, the setting of the derby enhances its status as one of the most anticipated fixtures in world football.

Iconic Encounters and Defining Moments

Over the decades, the Milan Derby has produced moments that have become the stuff of legend. Matches have been punctuated by breathtaking goals, dramatic comebacks, and tactical masterclasses that have altered the course of seasons. One such memorable encounter saw a late, thunderous strike that secured a dramatic win, leaving the stadium in stunned silence before erupting into euphoric celebration. These high-stakes moments are meticulously etched in the annals of football history, celebrated by both clubs' supporters and often serving as defining chapters in their respective narratives.

Each derby is a mosaic of individual heroics and collective effort. Whether it's the artistry of a forward weaving through defenders or the resolute performance of a goalkeeper defying the odds, the match is a showcase of talent, determination, and the indomitable spirit of Milanese football.

The Passionate Fanbases

The fervor of the Milan Derby is perhaps best encapsulated in the voices of its supporters. The fans of Inter and AC Milan are not merely spectators; they are active participants in a ritual that has been refined over generations. Their loyalty is visible in the sea of blue and red—colors that symbolize not only their club's identity but also the dreams and memories of countless supporters.

Inter fans, with their trademark passion and intensity, celebrate the club's fighting spirit and hard-earned successes. AC Milan's followers, on the other hand, take immense pride in their club's tradition of elegance, both on and off the pitch. On derby day, these passionate communities converge to create an atmosphere that is both electrifying and unpredictable, where every chant, banner, and burst of celebration reinforces the deep-rooted love for their team.

The Modern Era: Evolution and Innovation

In recent years, the Milan Derby has evolved to reflect the broader changes in modern football. Advances in tactics, sports science, and media coverage have all played a role in shaping the contemporary face of the rivalry. Yet, amid these transformations, the core essence of the derby remains unchanged—a relentless pursuit of excellence and an unwavering connection to the city's rich heritage.

Today, both clubs continue to innovate on and off the pitch. From the incorporation of cutting-edge technology to new strategies that balance tradition with modernity, Inter and AC Milan are committed to preserving the spirit of the derby while embracing the future of the sport. This delicate balance between honoring the past and forging new paths ensures that the rivalry remains as vibrant and relevant as ever.

Looking Forward

As the Milan Derby continues to captivate fans around the world, its future promises new chapters of drama, brilliance, and unforgettable moments. With each match, the rivalry is reborn, carrying forward a legacy that transcends generations and geographical boundaries. For the people of Milan, the derby is an enduring testament to the power of sport to unite communities, evoke deep emotions, and create memories that last a lifetime.

In celebrating the Milan Derby, we recognize not only the fierce competition between two great clubs but also the cultural and historical tapestry that enriches every encounter. It is a celebration of Milan's unique spirit—a city where football is an art form, and every match is a masterpiece painted with passion, history, and the relentless pursuit of glory.

Chapter 12: Derby Spotlight – The Rome Derby (AS Roma vs. Lazio)

Few rivalries in football evoke as much passion and political nuance as the Rome Derby, the fierce contest between AS Roma and Lazio. This clash is not simply about two clubs vying for supremacy—it is a microcosm of Rome's complex cultural, social, and political tapestry. In the Eternal City, where history echoes from every stone, the derby stands as an enduring symbol of local pride, identity, and a battle of contrasting visions for the city's future.

The Historical Backdrop

The roots of the Rome Derby extend deep into the annals of Italian history. AS Roma was founded in 1927 as a unifying symbol of the city, created by merging several older clubs in a bid to consolidate Roman football under one banner. Lazio, established earlier in 1900, had already forged its own identity, steeped in tradition and passion. Over time, the evolution of these clubs has mirrored the development of Rome itself—from the remnants of a grand imperial past to a modern metropolis where ancient legacies collide with contemporary ambitions. This historical interplay forms the foundation of the derby, infusing each encounter with a sense of destiny and gravitas.

Cultural, Social, and Political Dimensions

The Rome Derby is a study in contrasts, reflecting the dual nature of the city. AS Roma is often seen as embodying the spirit of the working class, drawing support from a diverse, passionate fanbase that identifies with the struggle for everyday dignity. In contrast, Lazio's supporters are frequently associated with a more conservative outlook, and the club has at times been intertwined with political narratives that emphasize traditional Roman values and regional pride.

This dichotomy is more than a matter of sporting rivalry; it mirrors broader societal debates about identity, modernity, and the preservation of heritage in a rapidly changing world. On derby day, these tensions crystallize into a display of fervor and determination. Each chant, banner, and moment of elation or despair carries with it the weight of these cultural and political undercurrents, making the match a powerful reflection of Rome's collective psyche.

The Theatre of the Derby

Stadio Olimpico, the shared fortress of both clubs, becomes a crucible where passion and history converge. Its grand architecture, with stands that have witnessed decades of triumph and tragedy, serves as the perfect backdrop for the Rome Derby. As the stadium fills with a sea of red and white on one side and sky blue and white on the other, the atmosphere is electric—a palpable blend of anticipation, rivalry, and mutual respect.

The setting itself adds a layer of dramatic intensity to the encounter. Under the Roman sky, where ancient monuments silently testify to a bygone era, the modern spectacle of football takes on an almost mythic quality. Each match is an homage to the city's past and a declaration of its present, uniting fans in a shared moment of communal identity.

Iconic Moments and Legendary Encounters

Over the years, the Rome Derby has delivered moments that have become the stuff of legend. From stunning individual performances and last-minute winners to tactical masterclasses that shifted the momentum of entire seasons, the derby has continually reinvented itself. Matches are often decided by the finest of margins—a solitary goal, a heroic save, or an unexpected twist in the narrative that sends shockwaves through the stands.

One unforgettable encounter saw AS Roma secure a

dramatic victory in the dying minutes of the match, sparking euphoric celebrations among its supporters and leaving Lazio's faithful in stunned silence. Such moments, etched into the collective memory of Rome's football community, serve as milestones in the rivalry's storied history and fuel endless debates among fans about strategy, destiny, and the unpredictable nature of the game.

The Role of the Supporters

The heart and soul of the Rome Derby lie in its supporters. The fans of AS Roma and Lazio are far more than mere spectators—they are passionate custodians of their clubs' identities and histories. On derby day, the streets of Rome come alive with the fervor of millions, as chants, songs, and colorful displays of support echo across the city. Family traditions are interwoven with personal memories, with each generation adding its own chapter to the ongoing saga of the derby.

For AS Roma supporters, the derby is a celebration of their resilience and the working-class spirit that has carried the club through both glory and hardship. Lazio fans, on the other hand, see the match as an assertion of their deep-rooted pride and a statement of their vision for the future. In the midst of the rivalry, there is an unspoken understanding—a shared recognition that, despite the fierce competition, both sets of fans are united by their love for the game and the city they call home.

Beyond the Pitch: The Derby's Wider Impact

The Rome Derby resonates far beyond the boundaries of the football field. It is an event that shapes local culture, influences social interactions, and even leaves an imprint on the political landscape of the city. The match has spurred countless artistic expressions—from murals and graffiti that capture the passion of the fans to literature and music that chronicle the emotions of derby day. Local businesses thrive on the influx of supporters, while media outlets and social platforms become arenas for spirited debate and communal storytelling.

This wide-ranging impact underscores the derby's role as a cultural phenomenon, one that encapsulates the complexities and contradictions of modern Rome. It is a reminder that football, in all its glory and unpredictability, remains a powerful force for unity and expression in a world of ever-shifting identities.

Looking Forward

As Rome continues to evolve, so too does the rivalry between AS Roma and Lazio. Modern football's demands—embracing technology, global broadcasting, and new tactical innovations—have added fresh layers to the derby's narrative without diluting its intrinsic passion. The future promises further evolution, with emerging talents, evolving strategies, and the enduring spirit of Roman pride ensuring that each encounter remains a moment of transcendence.

The Rome Derby is not just a match; it is a living testament to the city's past, present, and future. It captures the essence of what it means to be Roman—resilient, passionate, and eternally tied to a legacy that is as ancient as it is dynamic.

In celebrating the Rome Derby, we honor a spectacle that is far more than a sporting event. It is a vivid narrative of culture, identity, and history—a chapter in the endless story of Rome, where every match is a fusion of the old and the new, a timeless battle played out on a modern stage, and a powerful reminder of the unifying power of football.

Chapter 13: Derby Spotlight – The Lisbon Derby (Benfica vs. Sporting CP)

In the vibrant city of Lisbon, where the Tagus River kisses the Atlantic Ocean, football has long been the beating heart of local culture. But no fixture encapsulates the passion and intensity of this historic city quite like the Lisbon Derby, the fierce contest between Benfica and Sporting Clube de Portugal (Sporting CP). This rivalry is a blend of sporting excellence, social dynamics, and regional pride, making it one of the most heated and captivating rivalries in European football.

The Origins of the Rivalry

The roots of the Lisbon Derby stretch back to the early 20th century when both Benfica and Sporting were founded in a rapidly changing society. Sporting CP, established in 1906, quickly became associated with the elite of Lisbon, catering to a more affluent and aristocratic fanbase. In contrast, Benfica, founded in 1904, was born from the working-class districts of the city and quickly became the club of the people. Over time, the rivalry between the two clubs evolved not only on the football field but also as a reflection of Lisbon's social and economic divisions.

The two clubs' contrasting fanbases set the stage for a bitter rivalry. Sporting's historical association with the city's upper echelons and Benfica's connection to the working-class communities provided fertile ground for what would become a fierce and emotionally charged competition. The rivalry between Benfica and Sporting transcends the football pitch—each match is a symbolic contest for local supremacy, representing two distinct visions of Lisbon's identity.

Cultural Significance and Social Identity

The Lisbon Derby is not just a game; it is a celebration of identity, culture, and community. For Sporting supporters, the club represents a connection to Lisbon's aristocratic roots and the values associated with tradition, prestige, and social standing. The club's rich history in Portuguese football has solidified its position as one of the country's most respected institutions, and its fanbase reflects the club's sense of pride and tradition.

Benfica, on the other hand, is synonymous with the working-class neighborhoods of Lisbon. The club's identity is shaped by its blue-collar origins and its long-standing connection to the people of the city. Known as "The Eagles," Benfica has become a symbol of hope, resilience, and unity for the working class. Its fanbase is one of the largest in the country, and its supporters live and breathe the club's ethos of passion, community, and pride.

The Lisbon Derby, therefore, is not just a contest between two football clubs but an embodiment of the social, cultural, and economic divisions that have historically characterized Lisbon. On derby day, the atmosphere in the city is electric, with both sides gearing up for a match that is about far more than just three points. For Benfica and Sporting fans, victory in the derby is a matter of local pride, a chance to reaffirm the significance of their respective identities.

The Passion of the Fans

The intensity of the Lisbon Derby is matched only by the fervor of its supporters. Benfica and Sporting fans are known for their passionate and vocal support, with each club's fanbase creating an electric atmosphere on matchday. The rivalry between the two sets of supporters has produced some of the most memorable and dramatic moments in Portuguese football, and the rivalry's fervent atmosphere can be felt in every chant, cheer, and display of allegiance.

In the streets of Lisbon, the derby is a time for

celebration and tension alike. Fans from both sides don their team's colors, engage in friendly—yet often heated—banter, and fill the city's pubs and cafés to discuss tactics, recent form, and, of course, predictions for the derby. The passion of the supporters does not dissipate once the match is over; it lingers long after the final whistle, with each fan carrying the memory of the game for weeks or even months to come.

In the stands, both sets of supporters create an electric atmosphere that intensifies the action on the pitch. The sound of the crowd reverberates through the stadium as chants, songs, and synchronized displays of loyalty fill the air. These moments of collective expression—whether in moments of joy after a goal or in the tense silence that follows a missed opportunity—add to the drama and significance of the derby.

Iconic Moments and Historic Matches

Throughout the years, the Lisbon Derby has produced numerous iconic moments that have defined the rivalry and etched themselves into the history of Portuguese football. From last-minute goals to spectacular individual performances, these matches often feature a level of intensity that goes beyond mere competition.

One of the most legendary matches in recent history was

the 2009/2010 fixture, which saw Benfica and Sporting CP battle it out in a highly charged contest. Benfica, led by manager Jorge Jesus, were in excellent form, and a dominant 2-0 victory secured the bragging rights for the red side of Lisbon. The win not only gave Benfica local supremacy but also served as a significant boost to their title ambitions that season.

Another unforgettable moment came in the 1990s, when Sporting managed to dethrone Benfica in a dramatic derby, which was not only crucial for league standings but also a major psychological victory for Sporting's supporters. This match became a symbol of their resilience and their ability to challenge the dominance of their bitter rivals.

The frequent ups and downs of the derby ensure that every encounter is unpredictable, heightening the drama and making each match a unique spectacle in its own right. Whether it's the sheer tension or the stunning displays of footballing skill, the Lisbon Derby never fails to deliver high drama.

The Shared Stage: The Estádio da Luz and the José Alvalade Stadium

The rivalry is played out in two of Portugal's most iconic stadiums: Estádio da Luz, home to Benfica, and Estádio

José Alvalade, home to Sporting. These grand arenas are not just venues for sporting contests—they are hallowed grounds where legends are made and history is written.

Estádio da Luz, often referred to as the "Temple of Football," is a fortress for Benfica fans, a place where they expect nothing less than victory. With its imposing stands and vibrant atmosphere, it represents the heart and soul of Benfica. On derby day, it's a cauldron of noise and emotion, with the home fans roaring their team on, determined to maintain their status as the kings of Lisbon.

Estádio José Alvalade, on the other hand, is a symbol of Sporting's tradition, modernity, and ambition. Known for its impressive design and atmosphere, it is the stage where Sporting fans rally their team to defend their pride and seek victory. The green-and-white army fills the stadium with passionate support, making it a challenging environment for any visiting team, especially their arch-rivals, Benfica.

Both stadiums offer a unique setting for the derby, each amplifying the electric atmosphere that is so central to the Lisbon Derby's identity.

Looking Ahead: The Future of the Lisbon Derby

As Lisbon continues to evolve into a global city with a growing footballing reputation, the Lisbon Derby remains at the heart of the city's football culture. Modern football's demands—globalization, technology, and the commercial side of the sport—have changed the landscape of rivalries, but the essence of the Lisbon Derby remains unchanged. Benfica and Sporting will continue to battle for supremacy, not just for the city's pride but for their place in Portugal's footballing history.

With both clubs now consistently competing at the top of the league and investing in world-class talent, the derby is set to grow in prominence. The stakes will continue to rise, with each match carrying the weight of history and a fierce desire for local supremacy.

In the end, the Lisbon Derby is more than just a football match. It is a celebration of the city itself—a city of passion, history, and unyielding pride. Through every contest, every clash, and every goal, the rivalry between Benfica and Sporting CP tells a story of two great clubs, two fanbases, and one extraordinary city.

Chapter 14: Derby Spotlight – The Istanbul Derby (Fenerbahçe vs. Galatasaray)

In the vibrant and historic city of Istanbul, where continents collide and cultures blend, there exists a football rivalry that stands as one of the most intense and emotionally charged in the world. The Istanbul Derby, between Fenerbahçe and Galatasaray, is not simply a match—it is a war of identities, a battle for supremacy, and a microcosm of the city's rich, complex history. With deep-rooted passions, a fierce sense of local pride, and an unyielding desire for dominance, this derby transcends sport and becomes a statement of cultural, political, and social power.

The Origins of the Rivalry

The rivalry between Fenerbahçe and Galatasaray can be traced back to the late 19th century, a period when both clubs were founded as part of the rise of modern football in Turkey. Fenerbahçe, founded in 1907, emerged from the heart of Istanbul's Kadıköy district, which has long been considered a symbol of Istanbul's more cosmopolitan and, at times, conservative identity. Galatasaray, founded in 1905 by students from the prestigious Galatasaray High School, developed its identity as a symbol of the city's elite, with a deeply rooted connection to Istanbul's European side, and the influential, progressive ideas that shaped the modernizing Ottoman Empire.

From these early days, the rivalry was marked by a clash of identities—Fenerbahçe representing the working class and the more traditionalist aspects of Istanbul, while Galatasaray was seen as the club of the intellectual elite and modernists. This clash of cultures, classes, and ideologies has only deepened over time, with the footballing rivalry mirroring the socio-political and cultural divides within Istanbul itself. As both clubs continued to grow, they became symbols of competing visions for Turkey's future—Fenerbahçe as a traditional powerhouse, and Galatasaray as a progressive force with global aspirations.

The Cultural Divide: Fenerbahçe vs. Galatasaray

The rivalry between Fenerbahçe and Galatasaray is about far more than football—it is rooted in the city's complex cultural and social landscape. The fans of both clubs view the derby as a symbolic representation of their identity. Fenerbahçe's supporters often identify with the more conservative, working-class aspects of Istanbul, particularly from the Asian side of the city. Their pride lies in the club's deep connection to the heart of Istanbul's everyday life, representing the passions and struggles of the people who work hard and live through the city's challenges.

On the other hand, Galatasaray's supporters traditionally see themselves as the representatives of the elite, educated, and progressive sectors of Turkish society. The club's roots at Galatasaray High School and its connections to the European side of the city imbue it with a sense of intellectual and cultural prestige. The clash between these two sides represents more than just a footballing contest; it is a reflection of Istanbul's social dynamics and the divisions that exist within Turkish society.

The Passion of the Fans

The fans of Fenerbahçe and Galatasaray are among the most passionate and dedicated in world football. Every derby is an explosion of sound, color, and emotion, as both sets of supporters bring the full force of their pride and loyalty into the stadium. The atmosphere surrounding the Istanbul Derby is electric, with thousands of fans arriving hours before the match to begin their celebrations, share stories, and anticipate the drama that will unfold.

Galatasaray's fans, known for their fierce loyalty and

unwavering support, create a fiery atmosphere at their home ground, the Türk Telekom Stadium, where their distinctive chants and songs reverberate throughout the stands. Their presence is a symbol of the club's identity as a team of champions with a rich legacy.

Fenerbahçe's supporters, equally passionate, create an equally intense environment at their home, the Şükrü Saracoğlu Stadium. Known for their unrelenting enthusiasm and deep-rooted support for their team, Fenerbahçe fans bring a sense of familial pride to the derby. The energy and fervor of both sets of supporters contribute to an atmosphere that is both electrifying and intimidating, where every pass, every tackle, and every goal is celebrated or mourned as if it were a matter of life and death.

The passion of the fans often spills over into the streets of Istanbul in the days leading up to the match. It is not uncommon to see groups of fans marching through the city, singing their club's anthem, or engaging in friendly, yet competitive banter as they prepare for the big day. The rivalry permeates daily life, and matchdays feel like a festival of rivalry, uniting fans in a celebration of their loyalty to their respective clubs.

Iconic Matches and Defining Moments

The Istanbul Derby is defined by its unpredictability, with each match offering a new chapter in the fierce rivalry. Over the years, the derby has produced some of the most dramatic and intense moments in Turkish football history. Last-minute goals, stunning comebacks, and controversial incidents have all played their part in the derby's lore.

One of the most iconic moments came in 1996, when Fenerbahçe defeated Galatasaray 2-1 in the Turkish Cup final. The game was an emotional rollercoaster, with Fenerbahçe securing a dramatic win and its fans celebrating fiercely, while Galatasaray's supporters were left in despair. This match became a symbol of Fenerbahçe's resilience and determination, proving that the club could fight for glory on the biggest stages.

Another unforgettable moment occurred in 2001 when Galatasaray won 3-0 in a dominant performance that left Fenerbahçe fans speechless. This match was pivotal not only in terms of the scoreline but also in how it highlighted Galatasaray's rising prominence in Turkish football. The dominant performance became part of a larger narrative in which Galatasaray asserted itself as one of the top clubs in Europe, further intensifying the rivalry with Fenerbahçe, who were determined to reclaim their place at the top of Turkish football.

Such matches become ingrained in the collective memory of both fanbases, fueling the narrative of the rivalry and ensuring that every derby carries the weight of history, passion, and personal stakes.

The Role of the Stadiums

The two iconic stadiums of the Istanbul Derby—Şükrü Saracoğlu and Türk Telekom Stadium—serve as the battlegrounds where this bitter rivalry is brought to life. Şükrü Saracoğlu, home to Fenerbahçe, is known for its intimidating atmosphere, where the fans create an aura of tension and fervor that drives their team forward. The stadium is often referred to as a "fortress" for Fenerbahçe, a place where the club has achieved countless memorable victories.

On the opposite side, Türk Telekom Stadium, home to Galatasaray, is no less daunting. The club's supporters pack the stadium with relentless energy, and the atmosphere inside is nothing short of electric. The stadium's design and acoustics amplify the chants and songs of the Galatasaray faithful, making it one of the most intimidating venues for any visiting team.

Both stadiums, filled with the passion and pride of their

respective supporters, transform into arenas of intense emotion. The fans' energy creates an atmosphere where every moment of the match is heightened, every goal is celebrated or mourned with the utmost intensity, and the stakes feel larger than life.

The Future of the Istanbul Derby

As Turkish football continues to evolve in the modern era, the Istanbul Derby remains one of the most thrilling and fiercely contested rivalries in world football. With the rise of new stars, the increasing importance of global television broadcasts, and the ongoing development of the Turkish football infrastructure, the rivalry is poised to continue for years to come.

Both Fenerbahçe and Galatasaray are continually investing in their squads, strengthening their positions domestically and internationally. This ongoing development promises that each derby will be more competitive and more thrilling than the last, ensuring that the Istanbul Derby retains its status as one of the world's most intense and exciting football rivalries.

In celebrating the Istanbul Derby, we recognize more than just two clubs competing for supremacy. We acknowledge a deep-seated cultural and historical conflict that is played out on the football field but is felt throughout Istanbul and beyond. It is a rivalry that binds together generations of supporters, creates unforgettable moments of joy and heartbreak, and continues to shape the identity of Turkish football. Through every goal, every tackle, and every second of drama, the Istanbul Derby remains a testament to the enduring power of sport to unite, divide, and inspire.

Chapter 15: Derby Spotlight - The Superclásico (Boca Juniors vs. River Plate)

In the bustling streets of Buenos Aires, where passion and tradition intertwine, few spectacles capture the city's heart and soul like the Superclásico—the fierce football rivalry between Boca Juniors and River Plate. This derby transcends mere sport; it is a vivid tapestry woven with threads of history, culture, and unyielding local pride.

Origins and Historical Context

The roots of the Superclásico stretch back to the early 20th century, emerging from the vibrant La Boca neighborhood of Buenos Aires. Boca Juniors was established in 1905 by a group of Italian immigrants, adopting the club colors inspired by the flag of a Swedish ship that frequented the port. River Plate, founded in 1901, began in the same working-class district but relocated to the affluent Núñez area in 1925. This move sparked debates about abandoning humble origins, adding layers to the rivalry's narrative.

The term "Superclásico" combines "clásico," meaning derby, with "super," highlighting the immense stature of this matchup in Argentine football. Both clubs command the allegiance of over 70% of the nation's football fans, underscoring the derby's significance.

Cultural Significance and Social Identity

The Superclásico is more than a football match; it is a reflection of Buenos Aires' social and cultural fabric. Boca Juniors is often seen as the club of the people, representing the working-class ethos of the La Boca neighborhood. In contrast, River Plate is associated with the city's elite, symbolizing sophistication and affluence. This dichotomy fuels the rivalry, making each encounter a battle for social and cultural supremacy.

Iconic Stadiums and Electric Atmosphere

The stage for this epic rivalry is set in two iconic stadiums: La Bombonera, home to Boca Juniors, and El Monumental, the fortress of River Plate. La Bombonera, nestled in the heart of La Boca, is famed for its intimate atmosphere, where fans are close to the action, creating an electrifying environment. El Monumental, located in Núñez, boasts a vast capacity, hosting some of the most memorable clashes in football history.

On match day, these stadiums transform into cauldrons of emotion. The streets leading to the grounds are flooded with fans donning their team's colors, singing anthems, and engaging in passionate debates. The air is thick with anticipation, as both sets of supporters believe fervently in their team's destiny to triumph.

Legendary Matches and Defining Moments

Throughout the decades, the Superclásico has delivered moments that are etched into the collective memory of football fans worldwide. One such moment was the 2018 Copa Libertadores final, where the first leg at La Bombonera ended in a 2-2 draw. The return leg, initially scheduled for El Monumental, was relocated to Madrid's Santiago Bernabéu Stadium following incidents of violence, including an attack on Boca's team bus. This match, won by River Plate, is often cited as one of the most dramatic in football history.

The Global Allure

The Superclásico's allure extends beyond Argentina's borders. It has been featured in numerous documentaries, articles, and discussions, often highlighted as a must-experience event for football enthusiasts. The intensity, passion, and unpredictability of the match captivate audiences worldwide, solidifying its status as one of the greatest football rivalries.

Conclusion

The Superclásico between Boca Juniors and River Plate is more than just a football match; it is a celebration of

Buenos Aires' rich history, cultural diversity, and the unbreakable spirit of its people. Each encounter adds a new chapter to this ongoing saga, ensuring that the rivalry remains a defining feature of Argentine culture and a spectacle cherished by fans around the globe.

For a visual glimpse into the fervor of the Superclásico, you might find this video insightful:

Chapter 16: Derby Spotlight – The Catalan Derby (Barcelona vs. Espanyol)

In the vibrant, cosmopolitan heart of Catalonia, football is more than a pastime—it is an expression of identity, culture, and the fierce spirit of a people. The Catalan Derby, pitting Barcelona against Espanyol, encapsulates this passion. While Barcelona has grown into a global brand synonymous with artistry and success, Espanyol represents a proud local tradition and resilience. Together, they stage a contest that is as much about cultural pride as it is about the beautiful game.

Historical Foundations and Rival Identities

The roots of the Catalan Derby extend deep into the early 20th century. FC Barcelona, founded in 1899, quickly evolved into an emblem of Catalan nationalism and progressive ideals. From its humble beginnings in a small gymnasium, the club grew into a symbol of defiance and pride during times of political oppression, becoming a beacon for Catalan identity. In contrast, RCD Espanyol, established in 1900, developed along a different trajectory. While it always maintained strong local connections, Espanyol's identity has been tied to the everyday people of the city, reflecting the working-class spirit of a distinct section of Barcelona.

This divergence in origins has set the stage for a rivalry where each club represents contrasting visions of the region. Barcelona's emphasis on flair, innovation, and international ambition is counterbalanced by Espanyol's steadfast commitment to local tradition, community values, and a scrappy, determined approach on the pitch. The resulting clashes are as much a battle of philosophies as they are a contest of skill and strategy.

Cultural Resonance and Regional Pride

Football in Catalonia has long been interwoven with the region's struggle for autonomy and cultural expression. For FC Barcelona supporters, the derby is an opportunity to reaffirm not only their club's global stature but also their deep-rooted pride in Catalan heritage. The club's motto, "Més que un club" ("More than a club"), encapsulates the sentiment that football is intertwined with the fight for identity and self-determination.

Espanyol, while sometimes seen as the underdog, commands the loyalty of a passionate fanbase that cherishes its long history and local ties. The club's supporters take pride in their resilience and the undercurrent of authenticity that sets them apart. For them, the derby is not merely a contest against a global powerhouse—it is a declaration that local pride and tradition can stand up against even the most dominant forces in football.

The Stage: Nou Camp and RCDE Stadium

The settings for the Catalan Derby add to its drama and allure. FC Barcelona's Nou Camp is not only one of the world's most iconic stadiums but also a monument to the club's illustrious history and its role as a cultural institution. On derby day, the stadium fills with an electric mix of anticipation and pride, with chants and songs echoing the spirit of Catalan defiance and celebration.

In contrast, Espanyol's RCDE Stadium (and their previous home grounds) offers an intimate, passionate atmosphere where every supporter's voice is heard. The venue, modest in size compared to the Nou Camp, transforms into a cauldron of emotion when the derby arrives, reflecting the close-knit community that supports the club. The interplay between the expansive grandeur of Barcelona's arena and the fervent intimacy of Espanyol's home adds an extra layer of intrigue to the derby.

Iconic Moments and On-Field Drama

The history of the Catalan Derby is dotted with moments of high drama and unforgettable encounters. Over the decades, the matches have featured last-minute winners, stunning displays of individual brilliance, and tactical battles that have kept fans on the edge of their seats. One particularly memorable clash occurred when a late goal snatched victory from the jaws of defeat, igniting jubilant celebrations among the Espanyol faithful and sparking intense debate among neutrals. Such moments underscore the unpredictable nature of the derby, where passion and tension combine to create an atmosphere that is electric and timeless.

Each encounter is not only a contest for points but a narrative in itself—an unfolding drama that captures the hearts of fans and writes new chapters in a long-standing rivalry. The blend of technical mastery and raw emotion on display during these matches has made the Catalan Derby a fixture that transcends sport, resonating deeply with all who call Catalonia home.

The Passion of the Fans

Central to the allure of the Catalan Derby is the unwavering passion of its supporters. Barcelona fans, known for their global reach and unwavering support, bring an air of sophistication and pride that reflects the club's illustrious heritage. Their chants and choreographed displays are not only a celebration of football but a reaffirmation of their cultural identity. Meanwhile, Espanyol supporters, often fiercely loyal despite the club's underdog status, display an intensity that speaks to the club's deep local roots. Their fervor is palpable from the stands to the streets, as the derby becomes a communal event where every cheer and every tear carries the weight of history.

For both sets of fans, the derby is an annual rite—a time when differences are set aside in favor of a shared celebration of what it means to belong to Catalonia. It is a spectacle where the joy of victory and the agony of defeat are experienced collectively, binding generations together in a tradition that is as passionate as it is enduring.

Looking Forward: The Evolving Legacy

As football continues to evolve in the modern era, the Catalan Derby remains a steadfast symbol of regional identity and cultural pride. Both clubs are adapting to the demands of a globalized sport while maintaining the traditions that have defined them for over a century. With new talents emerging and tactical innovations reshaping the game, each derby promises fresh narratives and unforgettable moments.

The future of the Catalan Derby is bright and filled with potential. While FC Barcelona's international success and Espanyol's local determination provide a dynamic contrast, the underlying passion that fuels every encounter ensures that the derby will remain a cornerstone of Catalan culture for generations to come. In an age where commercial pressures and global media coverage increasingly shape football, the heart of the derby—its ability to evoke deep emotions and embody a sense of place—remains unchanged.

Conclusion

The Catalan Derby is a celebration of everything that makes football beautiful: the clash of ideologies, the power of cultural identity, and the indomitable spirit of its supporters. It is a match where history is relived with every tackle, every goal, and every chant—a living testament to the enduring legacy of Catalonia. In every encounter between Barcelona and Espanyol, the past and present collide, crafting a spectacle that is as unpredictable as it is magnificent, and as fiercely local as it is universally admired.

In the end, the Catalan Derby is more than a football

match—it is a vibrant expression of a community's soul, a dynamic narrative that continues to evolve, and a celebration of the passion that unites Catalonia through the beautiful game.

Chapter 17: Derby Spotlight - The Madrid Derby (Real Madrid vs. Atlético Madrid)

Few rivalries in Spanish football encapsulate the spirit of Madrid quite like the clash between Real Madrid and Atlético Madrid. This intense derby is not only a battle for local bragging rights but also a profound reflection of contrasting club philosophies, historical identities, and diverse fan cultures that have defined the capital's footballing landscape.

Historical Context and Origins

The roots of the Madrid Derby run deep, emerging from early 20th-century developments when both clubs began carving out their distinct identities in Spain's bustling capital. Real Madrid, with its illustrious history and global appeal, evolved into a symbol of establishment success and international glamour. In contrast, Atlético Madrid built its reputation on resilience, passion, and a strong connection to the working-class neighborhoods of Madrid.

Over the decades, the rivalry intensified as both clubs experienced periods of dominance and challenges, each victory and defeat adding layers to a narrative steeped in local pride and competitive spirit. The derby quickly transcended its origins as a simple sporting contest, becoming a battleground where regional and even national identities were fiercely contested.

Contrasting Philosophies and Club Identities

At the heart of the Madrid Derby lies a study in contrasts. Real Madrid's legacy is defined by a tradition of excellence, with a history filled with European triumphs and a commitment to a style of play that blends individual brilliance with tactical discipline. Often associated with the "Galácticos" era, Real Madrid represents ambition and the pinnacle of global football success.

Conversely, Atlético Madrid is celebrated for its gritty determination, robust defensive organization, and a fighting spirit that resonates deeply with its supporters. The club's identity is built on overcoming adversity, often defying expectations to challenge the traditional power structures of Spanish football. This contrast is mirrored in the fan bases—while Real's supporters are renowned for their cosmopolitan outlook and international following, Atlético fans are known for their passionate, working-class roots and unwavering loyalty.

Tactical Battles and On-Field Drama

The Madrid Derby is a showcase of tactical innovation and intense physicality. Real Madrid typically leverages its attacking prowess and fluid, high-tempo play to dominate possession and create chances through individual skill. Atlético Madrid, on the other hand, is often lauded for its disciplined, counter-attacking approach, with a strong emphasis on defensive solidity and exploiting quick transitions.

Managers from both sides craft strategies that reflect their club's identity, making in-game adjustments crucial in response to shifting dynamics. The tactical duel is a key element of the derby's allure, with each match presenting a new chess match where split-second decisions can alter the course of history.

The Atmosphere and Iconic Venues

The grandeur of the Madrid Derby is amplified by its iconic venues. Real Madrid's Santiago Bernabéu Stadium, with its rich history and atmosphere of relentless ambition, contrasts sharply with Atlético's modern Wanda Metropolitano, a fortress of passion and resilience. On match days, these stadiums become cauldrons of emotion, where every cheer and every groan echoes the weight of history and the fervor of the fans.

The electric atmosphere in both arenas is a testament to the derby's significance. Whether through the synchronized chants of the Bernabéu crowd or the impassioned support in the Metropolitano, the fans are not just spectators but active participants in a drama that unfolds with every touch of the ball.

Iconic Moments and Defining Matches

Throughout its history, the Madrid Derby has produced moments that have become legendary. From last-minute goals that swung momentum to tactical masterclasses that have redefined Spanish football, each encounter adds a new chapter to this storied rivalry. Matches have been decided by razor-thin margins, and controversial decisions have fueled debates that echo long after the final whistle.

Memorable fixtures, such as high-stakes encounters in the Copa del Rey and decisive La Liga clashes, have cemented the rivalry's place in football lore. These iconic moments continue to inspire passionate discussions among fans and serve as benchmarks for future generations.

The Modern Era: Globalization and Commercialization

In recent years, the Madrid Derby has adapted to the evolving world of football. Global media coverage, advanced data analytics, and the digital revolution have transformed how the derby is experienced and analyzed. Despite these modern influences, the core of the rivalry remains untouched—rooted in a deep historical context and sustained by the unwavering passion of its supporters.

As both clubs expand their global brands, the derby continues to serve as a reminder of football's local soul. The interplay between commercial success and the preservation of tradition is a balancing act that defines the contemporary identity of the Madrid Derby.

Conclusion

The Madrid Derby is much more than a football match—it is a microcosm of Madrid's diverse identity, a stage where contrasting philosophies collide, and a celebration of the passion that defines Spanish football. Real Madrid and Atlético Madrid represent two sides of the same coin: one embodying glitz and global dominance, the other resonating with the resilience and spirit of the working class. Together, they create a rivalry that is as intellectually stimulating as it is emotionally charged.

Each derby is a reminder that while tactics, players, and fortunes may change, the enduring spirit of competition and community remains at the heart of football. The

Madrid Derby continues to captivate audiences worldwide, offering a timeless narrative of ambition, determination, and the eternal quest for glory.

Chapter 18: Tactics and Strategies on Derby Day

Derby matches demand more than raw passion and emotion—they require a calculated blend of tactical ingenuity and strategic planning. On derby day, the pressure is palpable, and managers, players, and support staff leave nothing to chance. In this chapter, we delve into the tactical nuances and strategic decisions that shape these fiercely contested encounters, revealing how a deep understanding of the game can turn the tide in one of football's most volatile settings.

The Manager's Game Plan

In a derby, the role of the manager is magnified. With history, pride, and intense rivalries hanging in the balance, managers must craft game plans that not only exploit the opponent's weaknesses but also neutralize the enemy's strengths.

- **Preparation and Analysis:** Weeks before the match, extensive video analysis and scouting reports form the backbone of a manager's strategy. By studying previous encounters, managers identify patterns—both in their own team and in the opposition.
- **Psychological Warfare:** Beyond technical analysis, derby tactics often involve psychological

elements. Managers may opt for motivational speeches or unconventional formations to unsettle the opposition, ensuring that their team is mentally as well as physically prepared.

- **Adaptive Strategies:** Given the unpredictable nature of derby matches, flexibility is key. A successful manager is ready to alter tactics mid-game, responding to changes in momentum or unexpected challenges from the rival team.

Formations and Tactical Setups

Derby matches often see managers opting for formations that offer both solidity and the potential for rapid transitions.

- **Defensive Solidity:** With emotions running high and counterattacks frequently occurring, a strong defensive structure is paramount. Teams might employ a compact 4-2-3-1 or 4-3-3 formation, ensuring that midfield and defensive lines are tightly knit to repel sudden surges.

- **Counter-Attack and Transition:** When the opportunity arises, rapid counter-attacks can catch opponents off-guard. Quick transitions from defense to offense—often facilitated by speedy wingers or incisive midfielders—are a hallmark of successful derby tactics.

- **Midfield Control:** Dominating the midfield is essential to dictate the pace of the game. By controlling central areas, teams can disrupt the opposition's rhythm and create space for creative plays, balancing defensive duties with offensive creativity.

Set-Pieces and Game-Changing Moments

In high-stakes derbies, set-pieces often become the deciding factor.

- **Corners and Free Kicks:** Meticulous rehearsals on set-piece routines can yield spectacular results. Teams invest significant time perfecting corner deliveries, free-kick strategies, and even short, unexpected plays that catch rivals off balance.
- **The Element of Surprise:** Innovative set-piece tactics—such as deceptive runs or surprising formations—can be the spark that ignites a match, turning a dead ball situation into a decisive moment.

Player Roles and Individual Brilliance

While collective strategy forms the core of derby tactics,

individual brilliance can often tip the balance.

- **Key Playmakers:** Star players are entrusted with the responsibility of unlocking tightly organized defenses. Their vision, dribbling ability, and passing accuracy become critical components in creating goal-scoring opportunities.
- **Defensive Leadership:** Equally, leaders at the back play a crucial role in maintaining structure under pressure. Their ability to organize the defense, intercept key passes, and initiate counterattacks underlines the importance of experience and composure in derby matches.
- **Dynamic Wing Play:** In derbies, the flanks can serve as the stage for moments of individual genius. Quick, skillful wingers or overlapping full-backs stretch the opposition, creating pockets of space that can be exploited with precise, incisive passes.

In-Game Adjustments and Real-Time Decision Making

Derby matches are unpredictable, and even the best-laid plans may need rapid adaptation.

- **Mid-Match Analysis:** Successful managers

monitor the game's tempo and adjust their formations or player roles accordingly. Whether by substituting a defensive midfielder for an extra attacker or by reinforcing the backline, these real-time adjustments are critical in responding to the evolving dynamics of the match.

- **Exploiting Opposition Weaknesses:** As the match unfolds, opportunities often arise to exploit a momentary lapse in the rival team's organization. Keen tactical awareness allows a team to capitalize on these opportunities, whether it's a gap in the defense or an overloaded flank.
- **Managing Emotions:** The charged atmosphere of derby day means that emotions can run high on both sides. Tactical discipline—ensuring that players remain focused and composed despite the intensity—is a crucial aspect of maintaining a strategic advantage throughout the match.

The Role of Technology and Data

Modern derby tactics have evolved with technological advancements.

- **Data Analytics:** Teams now leverage data analytics to uncover patterns in play, understand individual performance metrics, and tailor their strategies to exploit specific weaknesses in the opposition.

- **Video Analysis:** High-definition footage and real-time analysis software enable managers to review and adjust their tactics swiftly, ensuring that the team remains a step ahead in the tactical battle.
- **Communication Systems:** Advanced communication systems allow managers to relay instructions to key players during the match, facilitating seamless in-game adjustments and ensuring that tactical shifts are implemented promptly.

Conclusion

The tactics and strategies employed on derby day are a blend of art and science—where preparation meets improvisation, and where the calculated execution of a well-crafted game plan intersects with the unpredictable nature of sport. In the high-stakes environment of a derby, every decision, formation tweak, and set-piece routine is imbued with the potential to change the course of the match. As managers and players navigate the complexities of these encounters, their ability to adapt, innovate, and remain composed under pressure ultimately defines the legacy of derby day.

In understanding the tactical depth of these storied encounters, we gain insight into the strategic heart that beats behind every pass, every tackle, and every moment of brilliance on the field. This chapter, dedicated to the meticulous planning and rapid-fire decision making that characterize derby matches, celebrates the cerebral side of football—a reminder that behind every display of passion, there is an equally compelling battle of minds.

Chapter 19: Derbies in the Digital Age

In the era of smartphones, social media, and real-time data, the landscape of football—especially the realm of derby matches—has been transformed. The digital revolution has redefined how fans engage with the game, how narratives are constructed, and how rivalries are experienced both inside and outside the stadium. In this chapter, we explore how modern technology has reshaped the derby experience, amplifying its drama, expanding its reach, and deepening its cultural impact.

The Rise of Social Media and Fan Engagement

Social media platforms have become the modern megaphones for fans worldwide.

- **Instant Reactions and Live Updates:** During derby days, platforms like Twitter, Instagram, and Facebook burst into life with live commentary, instant replays, and behind-the-scenes glimpses. Fans from every corner of the globe contribute to an ongoing digital conversation, sharing their excitement, frustrations, and celebrations in real time.
- **User-Generated Content:** Memes, videos, and personal stories flood timelines, transforming individual experiences into a collective digital

tapestry. The democratization of content means that every supporter has a voice, adding layers to the derby's narrative that extend far beyond the final whistle.

- **Hashtag Campaigns and Viral Moments:** Strategic hashtags and trending topics often emerge on match day, uniting supporters under a common digital banner. These campaigns not only amplify the derby's emotional impact but also help immortalize key moments in the rivalry's history.

Streaming and On-Demand Content

The way fans watch football has changed dramatically.

- **Global Accessibility:** High-speed internet and streaming services have made it possible for fans to watch derby matches live, regardless of geographical location. This global accessibility has broadened the fan base, turning local rivalries into worldwide phenomena.

- **Enhanced Viewing Experiences:** With multiple camera angles, instant replays, and interactive statistics, viewers can now dive deep into the tactical intricacies of a derby. Augmented reality (AR) and virtual reality (VR) technologies are beginning to offer immersive experiences that allow fans to feel as if they are in the stadium, experiencing the match from every perspective.

- **On-Demand Analysis:** Post-match analyses, expert breakdowns, and fan reaction videos are readily available on platforms like YouTube and dedicated sports apps. This on-demand content provides a richer, more nuanced understanding of the game, ensuring that the derby's narrative continues long after the match has ended.

Digital Storytelling and Multimedia Narratives

Derby narratives have evolved to include diverse forms of digital storytelling.

- **Documentaries and Mini-Series:** Platforms like Netflix and Amazon Prime now host documentaries that delve into the history, drama, and cultural significance of some of the world's most storied rivalries. These productions capture archival footage, personal interviews, and expert insights, offering fans a comprehensive look at the evolution of derbies.
- **Interactive Platforms:** Online forums, blogs, and interactive websites allow fans to share their memories, debate controversial decisions, and

even contribute to collective timelines of historic matches. This crowd-sourced narrative building creates a living archive that is constantly updated and enriched by multiple perspectives.

- **Podcasts and Live Chats:** The rise of football podcasts and live digital chats enables fans to engage in real-time discussions with pundits, former players, and other supporters. These platforms provide an intimate space for exploring the emotional and tactical dimensions of derby matches, adding depth to the digital discourse surrounding the game.

The Impact on Club Strategies and Marketing

Digital technology has also influenced how clubs approach derby matches from a commercial and strategic perspective.

- **Enhanced Fan Interaction:** Clubs now use apps and social media channels to interact directly with fans, launching exclusive content, behind-the-scenes access, and interactive features during derby days. This digital intimacy strengthens fan loyalty and deepens the emotional connection between the club and its supporters.
- **Data-Driven Marketing:** The wealth of data

generated by digital interactions allows clubs to tailor marketing campaigns, merchandise offers, and matchday experiences to individual fan preferences. By analyzing social media trends, clubs can predict the most engaging content and optimize their digital presence around the derby.

- **Virtual Community Building:** Digital platforms foster virtual fan clubs and online communities that transcend physical boundaries. These communities not only celebrate the derby's highs and lows but also serve as hubs for organizing viewing parties, charity events, and local meet-ups, thereby reinforcing the communal spirit that defines the rivalry.

The Future: Integrating Tradition with Innovation

As technology continues to advance, the digital transformation of derby experiences shows no signs of slowing down.

- **Artificial Intelligence and Predictive Analytics:** AI-driven insights are beginning to shape game-day strategies and fan engagement, offering predictive analytics that can forecast match outcomes and individual performances. This integration of data and intuition will add a new layer of intrigue to derby rivalries.

- **Virtual Reality Experiences:** VR promises to bring fans even closer to the action. Imagine experiencing a derby match as if you were sitting in the front row or even on the pitch with your favorite team. These immersive experiences will redefine what it means to be a football fan.
- **Blockchain and NFTs:** Emerging technologies like blockchain and non-fungible tokens (NFTs) are set to transform the memorabilia market, allowing fans to own unique digital artifacts—such as moments from historic derbies—that have both sentimental and monetary value.

Conclusion

The digital age has revolutionized every aspect of the derby experience, from how matches are watched and discussed to how clubs connect with their fans and market their brand. In this brave new world, tradition and innovation are not mutually exclusive; they coexist to create a richer, more dynamic narrative that honors the past while embracing the future. As digital technologies continue to evolve, the spirit of the derby—its passion, its drama, and its cultural significance—will only grow stronger, ensuring that the rivalry remains as compelling and transformative as ever.

In celebrating the digital transformation of derby matches, we acknowledge a profound truth: while the tools and platforms may change, the heartbeat of football—the raw emotion, the strategic brilliance, and the timeless narratives—remains constant, uniting fans across the globe in a shared celebration of the beautiful game.

Chapter 20: Economic and Commercial Impact

Football derbies are not just spectacles of sporting excellence—they are powerful economic engines that drive significant revenue streams, impact local businesses, and shape the broader financial landscape of the clubs and cities involved. In this chapter, we delve into the economic and commercial dimensions of football derbies, exploring how these high-stakes contests generate massive financial value both directly and indirectly. From ticket sales and broadcasting rights to merchandise and tourism, derbies are cornerstones of the modern football economy.

Matchday Revenues: The Financial Power of a Derby

A derby match is a goldmine for the host club, with revenue streams that are multiplied by the intense demand for tickets, hospitality packages, and matchday experiences.

- **Ticket Sales and Stadium Revenue:** The sheer demand for tickets to derby matches often leads to sell-out crowds, with the cost of admission for high-profile games commanding premium prices. Clubs leverage this demand by offering exclusive seating options, VIP packages, and corporate hospitality, which add significant revenue to matchday earnings.

- **Corporate Sponsorships and Partnerships:** Corporate sponsors are keen to associate their brands with the spectacle of a derby. Companies across various industries—from telecommunications and banking to retail and energy—often pay substantial sums to advertise in stadiums, on players' kits, and during televised broadcasts. These sponsorship deals are particularly lucrative during derby days, given the heightened visibility and media attention.
- **Matchday Hospitality:** Offering VIP boxes, premium lounges, and special fan experiences, clubs generate substantial revenue from hospitality services. These packages often include exclusive catering, behind-the-scenes access, and prime viewing locations, enhancing the overall derby experience for corporate clients and high-net-worth individuals.

Broadcasting Rights: The Global Reach of Derbies

In the digital age, the broadcasting of derby matches has become one of the most significant revenue streams for football clubs.

- **Television Rights and Broadcast Deals:** Broadcast rights for derby matches are worth millions of dollars, as these games attract not only local but also international audiences. Broadcasters—both national and global—compete for the right to air these high-profile encounters. The allure of derby day is immense, as millions of viewers tune in to watch the drama unfold.
- **Streaming and Digital Content:** With the rise of streaming platforms such as Amazon Prime, ESPN+, and DAZN, clubs and leagues have begun to explore new ways to monetize derby matches through digital distribution channels. Online streaming offers greater accessibility to global fans who may not have access to traditional television broadcasts, allowing clubs to tap into new markets and generate additional revenue.
- **International Audiences:** The global appeal of football has made derby matches a key driver of international fan engagement. The worldwide broadcasting of derbies brings fans from across the globe closer to the action, and their consumption of matchday content—whether

through live broadcasts, match highlights, or post-match analysis—generates substantial revenue through advertising, subscriptions, and syndication deals.

Merchandising and Product Sales

The economic impact of a derby extends well beyond the matchday itself.

- **Club Merchandise:** Derby matches are a goldmine for merchandise sales, as fans eagerly purchase jerseys, scarves, hats, and other team-branded items to showcase their support. Limited-edition products, such as special derby-day kits or commemorative items, can see a significant spike in sales.
- **Shirt Sponsorship and Licensing:** The global reach of football derbies has made shirt sponsorship one of the most lucrative aspects of the football business. Major brands pay large sums to have their logos emblazoned on the jerseys of iconic clubs. These sponsorships become particularly valuable during high-profile derby matches, where the global audience enhances the exposure of the brand.

- **Official Team Stores and Online Sales:** In addition to physical stores at stadiums, clubs are increasingly relying on online shops to sell their merchandise, making it easier for fans around the world to purchase derby-related items. Online platforms have become vital revenue streams, allowing clubs to reach international audiences and fans who cannot attend the match in person.

Tourism and Local Economic Impact

The economic impact of a derby extends beyond the stadium, with significant benefits for local businesses and tourism.

- **Hotel Bookings and Accommodation:** The influx of fans traveling to attend derby matches brings a boost to the local hospitality sector. Hotels, hostels, and short-term rental platforms like Airbnb see significant spikes in bookings around derby matchdays. Fans traveling from out of town spend money on accommodation, meals, and transportation, contributing to the local economy.
- **Bars, Restaurants, and Cafes:** The local food and beverage industry thrives in the lead-up to and after the derby, with bars, restaurants, and cafes filled with fans enjoying pre-match

gatherings and post-match celebrations. The atmosphere around the stadiums and in nearby areas becomes a festival of excitement, further driving sales for local businesses.

- **Tourism and Cultural Influence:** For many international fans, attending a derby is a bucket-list experience. Cities that host major derbies, such as Barcelona, Milan, and Buenos Aires, attract tourists eager to immerse themselves in the football culture. These tourists spend money not only on match tickets but also on sightseeing, dining, and souvenirs, adding to the broader economic impact of the derby.

The Long-Term Financial Impact: Building a Brand

The long-term financial benefits of derby matches extend beyond immediate revenues.

- **Branding and Global Recognition:** The global exposure that comes with hosting and participating in a derby enhances the brand image of both clubs. As clubs continue to compete in prestigious international tournaments, such as the UEFA Champions League, their derby-day performances contribute to their broader branding efforts. International media coverage, endorsements, and sponsorships increase the club's visibility, leading to new revenue opportunities.

- **Youth Development and Community Engagement:** The financial success of derby matches allows clubs to reinvest in grassroots development, youth academies, and community programs. By fostering local talent and investing in the next generation, clubs ensure their long-term success while strengthening their connection with the community.

Conclusion

The economic and commercial impact of football derbies is a testament to the immense value these matches generate—both on and off the pitch. From ticket sales and broadcasting rights to merchandise and local business growth, the financial ecosystem surrounding derby day has grown into a multi-faceted industry that extends beyond the confines of football itself. As the world of football continues to evolve, the economic importance of derbies will only increase, reinforcing their status as a cornerstone of the global footballing landscape.

As we look to the future, it is clear that derbies will

continue to drive the financial success of clubs, cities, and industries. Their ability to unite communities, attract global audiences, and generate unprecedented levels of revenue underscores the profound impact these matches have on the modern football economy. Football derbies are not only about competition; they are about the business of sport, and their significance reaches far beyond the stadiums, transforming entire economies and shaping the financial landscape of the game.

Chapter 21: Innovation and Modern Challenges

As football continues to evolve in the 21st century, the traditional world of derby rivalries is facing an era marked by rapid technological innovation and complex modern challenges. From the integration of advanced technologies on the pitch to the evolving dynamics of fan behavior and commercial pressures off it, today's derbies are as much a battleground for innovation as they are for sporting excellence. This chapter explores how modern challenges and technological advancements are reshaping the landscape of football rivalries, and how clubs, governing bodies, and supporters are adapting to a new age.

Technological Innovations: Shaping the Game

Video Assistant Referee (VAR) and Decision-Making

In recent years, the introduction of the Video Assistant Referee (VAR) has dramatically altered the tactical and psychological dynamics of derby matches. By providing real-time video reviews, VAR aims to reduce controversial decisions and ensure fairness. However, its implementation has also sparked debates among fans and pundits.

- **Impact on Tactics:** Managers and players now prepare for the possibility of review decisions that can overturn game-changing moments. This has led to more cautious play in critical situations and, in some cases, a shift in the way teams approach set-pieces and penalty situations.

- **Fan Reception:** While many appreciate the increased accuracy, others argue that the pauses and interruptions disrupt the flow and emotional intensity that have long defined derby atmospheres.

Smart Stadiums and Enhanced Fan Experiences

Modern derbies are being transformed by the rise of smart stadium technology. Clubs are investing in state-of-the-art facilities that integrate digital connectivity, immersive experiences, and real-time data analytics.

- **Connectivity and Engagement:** High-speed Wi-Fi, mobile apps, and interactive displays allow fans to access live statistics, replays, and tactical insights during matches. This has enriched the in-stadium experience, fostering a more engaged and informed fanbase.

- **Sustainability and Security:** Innovations in stadium design not only enhance comfort and accessibility but also address modern challenges such as crowd management, energy efficiency, and improved security measures—factors that are crucial in ensuring safe and enjoyable derby experiences.

Data Analytics and Tactical Evolution

The digital revolution has ushered in a new era of data analytics in football. Managers now rely on detailed performance metrics, heat maps, and predictive models to craft their game plans.

- **In-Game Adjustments:** Real-time data helps managers make informed decisions, allowing them to adjust formations and strategies on the fly to counter opponents' strengths.
- **Player Development:** Data-driven insights are also revolutionizing training methods, with personalized performance analyses helping players improve both individually and as part of a cohesive unit. This fusion of technology and tradition is redefining the tactical fabric of modern derbies.

Off-Field Challenges: Globalization and Commercialization

The Commercial Pressures of Global Football

Derby matches today are no longer solely local affairs;

they are global events that attract millions of viewers worldwide. With this increased exposure come heightened commercial pressures.

- **Revenue Versus Tradition:** Clubs face the delicate balancing act of maximizing revenue through sponsorships, broadcasting rights, and merchandising, while still preserving the authentic spirit of the derby.
- **Brand Expansion:** The global market demands that clubs maintain a polished, internationally appealing image. This drive for commercialization sometimes clashes with the raw, unfiltered passion that traditionally characterizes local derbies, leading to debates over authenticity and identity.

Fan Culture in the Digital Age

While digital platforms have expanded the reach of derby rivalries, they have also introduced challenges in maintaining the genuine, grassroots connection between clubs and their supporters.

- **Social Media Dynamics:** Social networks have transformed the way fans interact and share their experiences, sometimes blurring the lines between supportive banter and toxic behavior.

The anonymity and scale of digital interactions can fuel heated exchanges that spill over into real-world conflicts.

- **Preserving Local Identity:** As clubs seek to appeal to a global audience, there is growing concern that the unique local flavor of traditional derbies may be diluted. Maintaining a connection to community roots, even as clubs embrace modernity, is a challenge that many clubs are actively trying to navigate.

Security and Safety in a Modern World

With the influx of global fans and the intensification of media scrutiny, ensuring the safety and security of derby matches has become increasingly complex.

- **Crowd Management:** Advanced surveillance systems, coordinated police efforts, and improved stadium infrastructure are essential to manage the large, often emotional crowds that attend derby matches.

- **Countering Hooliganism:** Despite technological advances, issues such as hooliganism and sectarian conflict still pose serious challenges. Clubs, leagues, and law enforcement agencies continue to work together to develop strategies that safeguard the integrity of the derby experience while preserving the passion of the fanbase.

Balancing Innovation with Tradition

At its core, the derby is a celebration of history, community, and identity. As modern challenges and innovations reshape the landscape of football, there is an ongoing dialogue about how best to preserve the soul of these rivalries.

- **Embracing Change:** Many clubs have successfully integrated cutting-edge technology and modern commercial strategies without losing sight of their heritage. Initiatives that focus on community engagement, heritage projects, and fan education programs help bridge the gap between tradition and innovation.
- **The Role of Governing Bodies:** Football authorities are increasingly called upon to establish policies that balance fairness, safety, and commercial interests. Transparent decision-making and proactive regulation are critical in ensuring that the evolution of the game benefits all stakeholders—from players and clubs to the passionate supporters who live for derby day.

Conclusion

The modern era of football is defined by rapid technological advances and complex challenges that extend far beyond the pitch. Derbies, with their rich histories and passionate rivalries, are at the forefront of this transformation. As clubs, fans, and governing bodies navigate these changes, the true challenge lies in embracing innovation while safeguarding the traditions that make derby matches a unique and irreplaceable cultural phenomenon.

In this age of digital connectivity, data analytics, and global commercialization, the enduring spirit of the derby continues to inspire—and remind us—that, at its heart, football is a celebration of community, passion, and the timeless joy of the beautiful game.

Chapter 22: A Look into the Future – Evolving Rivalries in a Changing World

As we stand at the crossroads of tradition and transformation, the future of football derbies promises to be as dynamic and unpredictable as their storied past. This chapter explores how evolving social, technological, and commercial forces will shape the rivalries of tomorrow. From the impact of globalization to shifts in fan culture and the integration of cutting-edge technology, we examine the trends that will redefine how derbies are experienced, celebrated, and remembered.

Globalization and the Expanding Fan Base

Football's global appeal shows no signs of waning, and derbies are at the forefront of this worldwide phenomenon.

- **International Appeal:** With fans now spanning continents, rivalries that once held strictly local significance are gaining global traction. Television, streaming services, and social media platforms ensure that derbies are accessible to audiences far beyond their traditional geographic boundaries.
- **Cultural Exchange:** As international fans adopt

the chants, rituals, and traditions of their adopted clubs, new narratives emerge. The blend of local pride with global enthusiasm offers a fresh lens through which the classic rivalries are reinterpreted, creating a hybrid culture that honors heritage while embracing diversity.

- **Digital Communities:** Online forums and virtual fan clubs are uniting supporters from around the world, fostering discussions that not only celebrate the game but also reshape the identity of the derbies. This cross-cultural dialogue is poised to influence how clubs market themselves and how fans connect on a deeper, more global level.

Technological Innovations and the Next Generation of Football

The rapid pace of technological advancement is revolutionizing every aspect of football, and derbies are no exception.

- **Enhanced Viewing Experiences:** Future matchdays may offer unprecedented immersion through virtual reality (VR) and augmented reality (AR). Fans could experience derby atmospheres as if they were in the heart of the action—whether from home or in-stadium—blurring the line between physical and digital engagement.

- **Artificial Intelligence and Predictive Analysis:** AI-driven insights will continue to evolve, influencing everything from tactical decision-making to fan interaction. Data analytics may soon predict game outcomes and even guide real-time coaching adjustments, making every derby not only a contest of physical prowess but also of technological mastery.
- **Interactive Platforms and Blockchain:** As digital collectibles and non-fungible tokens (NFTs) become more mainstream, fans might own unique moments from historic derbies, further deepening the emotional and financial ties between supporters and their clubs. Such innovations could transform how memories are shared and cherished, providing new revenue streams while preserving the legacy of the rivalry.

Shifting Fan Culture and the Redefinition of Tradition

The modern fan is more connected, vocal, and engaged than ever before, leading to shifts in traditional derby culture.

- **Social Media Dynamics:** The power of social media continues to democratize the narrative. Fans are not just spectators; they are co-creators of history. This digital empowerment will likely lead to more inclusive and diverse representations of rivalry, as grassroots voices gain prominence alongside established traditions.
- **Evolving Identities:** As younger generations bring new values and perspectives to the stands, clubs are re-examining what it means to belong. Efforts to combat toxicity, promote inclusivity, and celebrate diversity are expected to redefine the derbies, ensuring that they remain vibrant expressions of both local identity and progressive social change.
- **Hybrid Experiences:** The future of derby days may blend physical attendance with virtual experiences, allowing fans who cannot be present at the stadium to participate in live, interactive events. This hybrid model will enable clubs to maintain the intimacy of local rivalries while engaging a broader, more global community.

Balancing Commercial Success with Authenticity

While commercial imperatives drive much of modern football, the essence of a derby lies in its authenticity—a delicate balance that clubs must strive to maintain.

- **Sustainable Growth:** As clubs expand their global footprints, they face the challenge of balancing revenue generation with preserving the soul of their local heritage. Successful models will be those that integrate modern marketing strategies with community-focused initiatives, ensuring that the passion and authenticity of the derby remain intact.
- **Community Engagement:** Investment in local projects, youth academies, and fan-centric events will be crucial in safeguarding the traditions that define each rivalry. These initiatives not only nurture the next generation of talent but also reinforce the deep-rooted connection between a club and its supporters.
- **Ethical Commercialization:** The future calls for commercial strategies that respect the spirit of the derby. Transparent governance, ethical sponsorships, and fan-driven content will help maintain a sense of community while capitalizing on the commercial opportunities afforded by

globalization.

The Vision Ahead

As we peer into the future of football rivalries, one truth remains clear: while the tools, technologies, and global reach of the game may change, the heart of a derby—its passion, its drama, and its connection to community—will endure.

- **Continuity in Change:** Even as clubs adopt new technologies and expand their horizons, the timeless appeal of a derby remains rooted in shared history and collective emotion. Every match will continue to be a canvas on which the stories of communities are painted, capturing both triumph and heartbreak.
- **Adaptation and Resilience:** The evolution of derbies will depend on the ability of clubs, fans, and governing bodies to adapt to changing circumstances without losing sight of what makes the rivalry special. Balancing innovation with tradition will be key, ensuring that each derby remains a celebration of the beautiful game—one that resonates with both long-time supporters and new audiences alike.

Conclusion

The future of football derbies is a complex, multifaceted tapestry—one that weaves together the threads of global connectivity, technological innovation, evolving fan culture, and the ever-present drive for commercial success. In this changing world, derbies will continue to be a powerful expression of identity, passion, and community, even as they adapt to meet the demands of a modern era.

In celebrating the future of these iconic rivalries, we honor not only the enduring spirit of the derby but also the endless possibilities that lie ahead. The road forward is one of innovation, inclusivity, and balance—a journey that will shape the next chapter in the rich, ongoing saga of football's most passionate encounters.

Chapter 23: Conclusion – The Enduring Legacy of Derby Days

Football derbies have long transcended the boundaries of sport, imprinting themselves on the hearts and minds of communities worldwide. In this final chapter, we reflect on the timeless legacy of derby days—a legacy built on passion, history, and a shared sense of identity that continues to evolve with every match. As we close this exploration of fierce rivalries, we celebrate not only the drama on the pitch but also the cultural, social, and economic forces that have shaped the beautiful game.

A Tapestry of History and Emotion

At their core, derbies are living narratives—stories of triumph and heartbreak that have been woven into the fabric of local and global culture. Each match is a chapter in a larger saga:

- **Historical Echoes:** From the early days of industrial labor to modern urban battles, derbies capture the spirit of communities at different points in time. They serve as a reminder that football is as much about the people and their stories as it is about the sport itself.
- **Emotional Resonance:** The intensity of rivalry, the roar of the crowd, and the personal memories

forged in the heat of competition give these encounters an enduring emotional power that resonates across generations.

Cultural and Social Impact

Derbies have the unique ability to unite and divide, reflecting the complex dynamics of society:

- **Community Identity:** Whether it is the working-class pride of a local neighborhood or the sophisticated allure of a global brand, derbies reinforce community bonds and create a shared sense of belonging.
- **Art and Expression:** The influence of derby culture can be seen in art, music, literature, and even political discourse—an enduring reminder of how football transcends sport to become a mirror of society.
- **Legacy of Passion:** The chants, rituals, and traditions of derby days are passed down from one generation to the next, ensuring that the passion for the game remains vibrant and ever-evolving.

The Everlasting Influence on Modern Football

The legacy of derby days is not confined to history—it

continues to shape the modern game in profound ways:

- **Tactical Evolution:** Derbies have driven innovation in strategy and tactics. The high-pressure environment forces managers and players to evolve continually, influencing broader trends in the sport.
- **Economic Transformation:** The commercial success of derby matches has redefined the financial landscape of football. From ticket sales to global broadcasting deals, the economic impact of these games has fueled growth and inspired new business models.
- **Digital Renaissance:** In an era of digital connectivity, derbies have found new life on social media and streaming platforms. Fans around the world participate in a collective narrative, ensuring that the legacy of these rivalries remains dynamic and accessible.

A Future Steeped in Tradition and Innovation

As we look ahead, the future of derby days promises to be as captivating as their storied past:

- **Embracing Change:** New technologies and evolving fan cultures will continue to enrich the derby experience, blending tradition with innovation in ways that honor the past while forging new pathways for the future.

- **Global Community:** The universal language of football ensures that the legacy of derbies will remain a unifying force, connecting diverse cultures and communities across the globe.
- **Sustainable Passion:** Amid the rapid changes of modern sport, the core values of rivalry—passion, pride, and resilience—will endure. They are the heartbeat of the derby and the foundation upon which future legends will be built.

Final Reflections

Derby days are more than mere matches; they are a celebration of the human spirit—a testament to the power of sport to evoke deep emotions, bridge divides, and inspire hope. They remind us that, while the world may change, the fundamental thrill of a hard-fought contest remains timeless. Every goal, every cheer, and every moment of despair is etched into the collective memory of fans, ensuring that the legacy of derby days lives on.

In closing, this journey through the world of football derbies invites us to appreciate not just the rivalry on the field but also the intricate web of cultural, economic, and social forces that make these encounters truly extraordinary. As the final whistle blows on each derby, the echoes of passion continue to resonate—reminding us that football, in all its glory and complexity, is a celebration of life itself.

Welcome to the enduring legacy of derby days—a legacy that will inspire generations to come.

Appendix A: Timeline of Iconic Derby Moments

This appendix offers a chronological journey through some of the most unforgettable moments in the history of football derbies. From the earliest encounters that ignited local rivalries to modern-day clashes that have captivated millions, this timeline highlights pivotal events that have shaped the culture, passion, and legacy of derby football. Each entry not only marks a significant sporting milestone but also reflects the social, cultural, and emotional impact these matches have had on communities worldwide.

Late 19th Century – The Birth of Rivalries

- **1879 – Early Local Contests in England:**
  The roots of football rivalries begin to take shape in local matches among neighborhood clubs in industrial cities. These early fixtures set the stage for community-based competitions that would evolve into modern derbies.
- **1880s – Foundations of Community Football:**
  As clubs start to form in working-class communities, the passion for local pride is kindled. Early contests in cities like Glasgow and Manchester sow the seeds of what will become

legendary rivalries.

Early to Mid-20th Century – Establishing Traditions

- **1905 – The Founding of Boca Juniors:**
  In Buenos Aires, the birth of Boca Juniors marks the beginning of a rivalry that will eventually evolve into the celebrated Superclásico. The club's early days in La Boca help establish its identity as a symbol of working-class pride.
- **1913 – Arsenal's Move to North London:**
  Arsenal's relocation to Highbury ignites tensions with Tottenham Hotspur, setting the stage for one of the most fiercely contested derbies in English football. This move underscores how geography and identity can fuel rivalry.
- **1927 – The Formation of AS Roma:**
  Created as a unifying force for the city, AS Roma's establishment marks the beginning of a rivalry with Lazio that is deeply intertwined with Rome's social and cultural history.
- **1930s – The Rise of the Old Firm:**
  In Glasgow, the contrasting identities of Celtic and Rangers begin to crystallize. The 1930s see the

Old Firm derby evolve into a fixture that mirrors the deep-seated religious and cultural divides within Scotland.

Post-World War II – Moments That Defined Generations

- **1950s – The Merseyside Rivalry Deepens:**
  As football becomes the national passion in England, the Merseyside Derby between Liverpool and Everton takes on new meaning. Key matches during this period solidify the derby's reputation for intensity and local pride.
- **1960 – The Birth of Modern Football Tactics:**
  Tactical innovations start to change the way derbies are played. Matches begin to feature more organized structures, setting a new standard for the intensity and strategic complexity of rivalry games.
- **1970 – North London Battles Intensify:**
  The clashes between Arsenal and Tottenham reach fever pitch during the early 1970s, with several matches decided by narrow margins that are remembered for their dramatic finishes and lasting impact on fan culture.

Late 20th Century – Drama and Globalization

- **1980 – The Old Firm's Tactical Masterclasses:** Iconic matches in the 1980s between Celtic and Rangers showcase tactical brilliance and moments of individual heroism, further embedding the rivalry in Scottish cultural memory.
- **1991 – The North London FA Cup Semi-Final:** Tottenham Hotspur's thrilling 3-2 victory over Arsenal in the FA Cup semi-finals becomes a defining moment for Spurs, highlighting the derby's potential for dramatic upsets and lifelong memories.
- **1996 – Istanbul Derby Cup Final:** Fenerbahçe and Galatasaray clash in a dramatic Turkish Cup final, a match remembered for its nail-biting finish and the passionate response from fans on both sides—a moment that exemplifies the fierce nature of the Istanbul Derby.
- **Late 1990s – Superclásico Evolution:** The rivalry between Boca Juniors and River Plate reaches new heights as television and global

broadcasting begin to showcase the drama of the Superclásico to international audiences, cementing its status as one of football's greatest spectacles.

21st Century – The Digital Era and Contemporary Classics

- **2001 – The Rise of the Modern Derby:**
  In the new millennium, derbies such as the Manchester Derby evolve with the advent of advanced technology and global media coverage. Memorable matches during this period see last-minute goals and tactical shifts that define modern football rivalries.
- **2009/2010 – Lisbon Derby Brilliance:**
  The dramatic encounters between Benfica and Sporting CP during this season, including decisive victories and memorable comebacks, highlight how modern derbies can influence both league standings and local pride on a grand scale.
- **2018 – Superclásico Controversy:**
  A historic Superclásico in which River Plate's victory in the Copa Libertadores final—played under extraordinary circumstances following

security concerns—captures the volatile blend of passion, politics, and drama inherent in this legendary rivalry.

- **2020s – The Digital Transformation:**
  Recent derbies have been characterized by the integration of digital technology, with real-time social media interactions, instant replays, and data analytics adding new layers to the viewing experience. These innovations ensure that the drama of derby days is accessible to a global audience, reinforcing the timeless appeal of these contests.

Reflection

This timeline serves as a testament to the enduring power of football derbies. Each moment—whether celebrated for tactical brilliance, dramatic twists, or the raw emotion of the fans—has contributed to a rich tapestry that transcends the sport itself. The events listed here not only mark milestones in football history but also illuminate how derbies have become mirrors reflecting the changing social, cultural, and technological landscapes of our world.

By chronicling these iconic moments, we honor the

legacy of derby days and invite readers to appreciate the profound impact these rivalries continue to have on football and society at large.

Appendix B: Profiles of Legendary Derby Icons

This appendix pays tribute to the individuals whose brilliance, passion, and leadership have defined the legacy of football derbies. From players who lit up the pitch with unforgettable performances to managers whose tactical genius shaped historic matches, these profiles offer a glimpse into the lives and careers of the legends who transformed derby days into timeless spectacles. Each profile highlights key moments, personal anecdotes, and the enduring impact these figures have had on the rivalries that captivate millions around the world.

---

1. The Maestro of Merseyside: Kenny Dalglish

Clubs: Liverpool
Era: 1977–1990

Kenny Dalglish's name is synonymous with Liverpool's golden era. As both a prolific forward and a tactically astute manager, Dalglish was instrumental in turning the Merseyside Derby into a showcase of technical excellence and competitive spirit. His vision on the pitch and his ability to inspire teammates during high-pressure encounters elevated the derby to an art form. Dalglish's legacy is marked by his knack for delivering in clutch moments, earning him admiration from fans on both sides of the rivalry.

---

2. The Icon of North London: Glenn Hoddle

Clubs: Tottenham Hotspur
Era: 1975–1987

Glenn Hoddle's elegant playmaking and visionary passing redefined the North London Derby. A creative genius on the field, Hoddle's technical skills and ability to dictate the flow of the game made him a key figure for Tottenham Hotspur during intense derby battles against Arsenal. His style of play combined flair with precision, earning him accolades as one of the most influential midfielders of his generation. Beyond his on-field exploits, Hoddle's insights into the game later informed his managerial career, leaving a lasting impact on the tactical evolution of derbies.

---

3. The Spirit of Glasgow: Billy McNeill

Clubs: Celtic
Era: 1960s–1970s

As a stalwart leader and revered captain for Celtic, Billy McNeill embodied the fighting spirit of the Old Firm derby. His inspirational leadership and unwavering commitment on the pitch galvanized his teammates, particularly in matches that pitted Celtic against their fierce rivals, Rangers. McNeill's ability to lift his team in moments of adversity and his profound connection with the fans solidified his status as a legendary figure whose legacy is celebrated in every derby encounter.

---

4. The Tactical Innovator: Arrigo Sacchi

Clubs: AC Milan (as manager)
Era: Late 1980s–Early 1990s

Arrigo Sacchi revolutionized the way football was played, and his impact was profoundly felt during the Milan Derby. With AC Milan, Sacchi introduced a high-pressing, organized style that redefined defensive solidity and offensive fluidity. His innovative approach not only won trophies but also set new tactical standards for derby matches, influencing generations of managers. Sacchi's relentless pursuit of perfection and his ability to adapt strategies in real time continue to be studied by football aficionados around the globe.

---

5. The Heart of Buenos Aires: Diego Maradona

Clubs: Boca Juniors (short stint)

Era: Early 1980s

Though best known for his international exploits, Diego Maradona's time with Boca Juniors left an indelible mark on the Superclásico. Maradona's charisma, extraordinary dribbling skills, and unparalleled vision injected a new level of excitement into derby matches in Buenos Aires. His magnetic personality and on-field brilliance created moments of magic that resonated deeply with the Boca faithful. Maradona's influence in derby lore is a reminder of how a single player's genius can elevate the spectacle to legendary status.

---

6. The Maestro of Madrid: Sergio Ramos

Clubs: Real Madrid (rivalry with Atlético Madrid)

Era: 2005–2021

Sergio Ramos, with his fierce competitiveness and leadership, became the embodiment of the Madrid Derby's intensity. Known for his decisive goals and defensive prowess, Ramos played a pivotal role in Real Madrid's success during his tenure. His aggressive style and clutch performances in high-stakes matches against

Atlético Madrid have cemented his reputation as a derby hero. Ramos's legacy is characterized by his unyielding determination, which has inspired countless players and fans to appreciate the tactical and emotional depths of rivalry matches.

---

7. The Visionary: Johan Cruyff

Clubs: Ajax and Barcelona (influencing derby cultures)
Era: 1970s–1990s

Johan Cruyff was more than a player—he was a revolutionary thinker whose ideas transcended individual rivalries. His philosophy of Total Football transformed the tactical landscape of European football and left an enduring legacy in derby settings, particularly in Barcelona. Cruyff's innovative approach not only redefined his teams' playing styles but also influenced how derbies are approached tactically. His emphasis on fluidity, space, and collective movement continues to resonate, reminding fans and managers alike of the beauty and complexity of the game.

---

8. The Tenacious Defender: Paolo Maldini

Clubs: AC Milan

Era: 1984–2009

Paolo Maldini epitomizes defensive excellence and longevity in football. As a stalwart for AC Milan, his calm presence and exceptional reading of the game were crucial in some of the most intense Milan Derby clashes. Maldini's career is a masterclass in consistency, leadership, and technical brilliance on the defensive end. His ability to neutralize opposition threats and inspire his team through adversity makes him one of the most revered figures in the history of derbies, a true guardian of his club's legacy.

Reflection

The figures featured in this appendix have not only excelled individually but have also become integral threads in the rich tapestry of derby history. Their careers, marked by moments of genius, leadership, and unwavering passion, illustrate the profound influence that exceptional talent can have on the enduring appeal of football rivalries. As we reflect on their contributions, we gain a deeper understanding of how individual brilliance and collective spirit intertwine to create the magic of derby days.

Appendix C: The Cultural Mosaic of Derby Fandom

This appendix delves into the rich and diverse world of derby fan culture—a vibrant tapestry of rituals, chants, traditions, and artistic expressions that define the unique identity of each rivalry. Beyond the players and tactics, the soul of a derby is found in its supporters. Here, we explore the many facets of fan expression that make derby days a cultural phenomenon celebrated around the globe.

---

1. Chants, Songs, and Anthems

Derby fans are known for their passionate vocal displays, which serve both to inspire their teams and to intimidate their rivals.

- **Traditional Anthems:** Many clubs boast time-honored songs that are sung at every match, creating a sense of continuity and belonging. These anthems often reference historical achievements and local pride.
- **Improvised Chants:** During high-stakes moments, supporters spontaneously create chants to reflect the unfolding drama on the pitch. These impromptu expressions often capture the raw

emotion of derby day.

- **Rivalry Taunts:** A key element of derby culture is the playful yet fierce banter exchanged between opposing fans. Clever wordplay, humorous insults, and memorable refrains contribute to a unique verbal duel that adds to the match's excitement.

---

2. Rituals and Traditions

Across the world, derby supporters observe a variety of rituals that have been passed down through generations, reinforcing community bonds and preserving cultural heritage.

- **Pre-Match Gatherings:** In many cities, fans converge in local pubs, community centers, or even public squares hours before kickoff. These gatherings serve as both social events and warm-ups, where fans share stories, debate tactics, and build the collective energy for the match.
- **Scarf and Banner Displays:** Iconic club scarves and banners are more than mere accessories—they are symbols of loyalty and identity. The choreographed display of colors in the stands

often creates breathtaking visual spectacles that embody the spirit of the rivalry.

- **Superstitions and Rituals:** Many fans adhere to personal or communal superstitions—such as wearing a specific jersey, following a unique pre-match routine, or even observing silence during a crucial moment—to bring good luck and ward off bad fortune.

---

3. Art, Literature, and Media

Derby fandom extends well beyond the stadium, permeating various forms of creative expression that celebrate the rivalry.

- **Mural Art and Graffiti:** In many derby cities, walls and public spaces become canvases for artistic tributes to local clubs. Murals capture historic moments, iconic players, and the collective spirit of the fanbase, transforming urban landscapes into living galleries of support.
- **Fan Fiction and Poetry:** Inspired by the passion of derby days, numerous writers and poets have chronicled their experiences, crafting stories and verses that encapsulate the emotion and drama of

these encounters.

- **Documentaries and Podcasts:** Modern media platforms have given rise to an array of documentaries and fan-driven podcasts that explore derby culture from multiple angles. These productions provide in-depth analysis, behind-the-scenes stories, and personal interviews that deepen our understanding of what it means to be a derby supporter.

---

4. Global Communities and Digital Expression

The digital revolution has redefined fan culture, allowing supporters from around the world to unite and share their passion for derby football.

- **Online Fan Forums and Social Media:** Platforms like Twitter, Facebook, and dedicated fan forums enable fans to discuss matches, share memories, and debate controversial decisions in real time. The collective voice of the global fan community adds a new dimension to derby rivalries.
- **Virtual Viewing Parties:** In an increasingly connected world, virtual gatherings and online streaming events allow fans who cannot be

physically present to experience the derby atmosphere together. These digital meetups preserve the sense of community and shared excitement that is integral to the derby experience.

- **Digital Art and Memes:** Creativity flourishes in the digital age, with fan-made graphics, memes, and video montages capturing the essence of derby days. These expressions not only entertain but also serve as modern relics of football history, encapsulating key moments in a shareable format.

---

5. The Impact of Fan Culture on the Derby Experience

The cultural expressions of derby supporters do more than simply enhance the spectacle—they shape the very identity of the rivalry.

- **Emotional Resonance:** The chants, rituals, and artistic expressions of fans create an atmosphere that elevates the match from a mere contest to an emotional pilgrimage. Every cheer and every collective roar contributes to the unforgettable energy that defines derby days.

- **Community Identity:** Fan culture reinforces a sense of belonging and pride. Whether through traditional songs or modern digital art, these cultural expressions forge deep connections among supporters, binding them together across generations.
- **Legacy and Memory:** The creative output of derby fans helps preserve the history and legacy of these rivalries. Through art, literature, and digital media, the stories of derby days are passed on, ensuring that the passion and spirit of the rivalry endure long after the final whistle.

Reflection

This appendix highlights the multifaceted nature of derby fan culture—a vibrant mosaic of tradition, creativity, and modern innovation. It is a celebration of the voices that echo through stadiums, the art that adorns city walls, and the digital narratives that connect millions of supporters worldwide. In capturing the cultural essence of derby fandom, we gain insight into why these matches resonate so deeply with fans and continue to inspire passion across the globe.

Appendix D: Further Reading and Resources

For readers eager to delve deeper into the rich history, passionate culture, and evolving landscape of football derbies, this appendix provides a curated list of books, documentaries, websites, podcasts, and academic resources. These materials offer varied perspectives—from historical analyses to personal fan narratives—ensuring that enthusiasts can explore every facet of derby culture.

Books

- **"Fever Pitch" by Nick Hornby**
  A seminal memoir that captures the emotional highs and lows of being a devoted football fan. Hornby's narrative provides personal insights into how derby days shape identity and community.
- **"Inverting the Pyramid: The History of Football Tactics" by Jonathan Wilson**
  This comprehensive study delves into the evolution of football strategies and offers context for how tactical innovations have influenced derby matches over the decades.

- **"Soccernomics" by Simon Kuper and Stefan Szymanski**
  Combining economics with football, this book explores the financial and cultural dimensions of the sport, including discussions on high-stakes rivalries and their global impact.
- **"The Ball is Round: A Global History of Football" by David Goldblatt**
  A sweeping historical account of football's evolution, this book provides context for the socio-political forces that have shaped rivalries around the world.

Documentaries and Films

- **"Take the Ball, Pass the Ball" (2018)**
  A documentary offering behind-the-scenes insights into FC Barcelona's playing style, which has influenced the tactics of several derby teams.
- **"Ronaldo" (2015)**
  While focused on Cristiano Ronaldo, this film touches on the broader competitive landscape of football, including insights into high-pressure derby settings.

- **"The Two Escobars" (2010)**

  This documentary examines the intersections of sport, politics, and society in Colombia, offering a compelling look at how local rivalries can have far-reaching implications.

- **YouTube Channels:**

  Explore channels like *Tifo Football*, *COPA90*, and *Zonal Marking* for visually engaging analyses, tactical breakdowns, and historical retrospectives on famous derbies.

Websites and Blogs

- **FIFA and UEFA Official Websites**

  Official platforms providing match reports, historical archives, and expert analyses of international derbies and major tournaments.

- **Football Supporters' Forums (e.g., Reddit's r/soccer, The Football Forum)**

  Interactive communities where fans share personal experiences, debate historical moments, and provide real-time updates on derby matches.

- **Club-Specific Websites and Fan Blogs**

  Many clubs maintain official histories and fan-curated blogs that offer unique insights into derby-day traditions, memorable matches, and behind-the-scenes stories.

Podcasts

- **"Football Weekly" by The Guardian**
  A popular podcast featuring in-depth discussions, expert opinions, and fan perspectives on the latest derby matches and football news.
- **"The Football Ramble"**
  Known for its humorous and insightful take on football culture, this podcast often features discussions about the emotional and tactical aspects of major derbies.
- **"Tifo Football Podcast"**
  Offers tactical analyses and historical context, ideal for listeners who want to understand the nuances behind derby match strategies.

Academic and Research Articles

- **Journal of Sports Economics**
  Offers research articles on the financial impact of sports events, including studies on ticket pricing,

broadcasting rights, and merchandising related to high-profile derbies.

- **Sociology of Sport Journal**
  Features academic papers examining how football rivalries reflect and influence social identities, community cohesion, and cultural expression.
- **Digital Libraries and University Repositories**
  Institutions like JSTOR and Google Scholar host a range of articles on sports history, cultural studies, and the impact of digital media on fan culture—ideal for those seeking a more scholarly perspective.

Reflection and Exploration

This collection of resources is designed to serve as a gateway for further exploration into the multifaceted world of football derbies. Whether you're interested in the strategic innovations that define these matches, the passionate narratives of dedicated fans, or the broader socio-economic impacts on communities, these materials provide a wealth of knowledge and inspiration.

By engaging with these books, documentaries, websites, podcasts, and academic studies, readers can deepen their understanding of how derbies have shaped—and continue to influence—the global phenomenon of football.

www.ingramcontent.com/pod-product-compliance
Ingram Content Group UK Ltd.
Pitfield, Milton Keynes, MK11 3LW, UK
UKHW050014150425
5461UKWH00070B/412

9 781923 472143